Faith Secrets

Dag Heward-Mills

Parchment House

Unless otherwise stated, all Scripture quotations are taken from the
King James Version of the Bible

FAITH SECRETS

Copyright © 2018 Dag Heward-Mills

First published 2019 by Parchment House
1st Printing 2019

Find out more about Dag Heward-Mills at:
Healing Jesus Campaign
Write to: evangelist@daghewardmills.org
Website: www.daghewardmills.org
Facebook: Dag Heward-Mills
Twitter: @EvangelistDag

ISBN: 978-1-64329-226-7

All rights reserved under international copyright law. Written permission must be secured from the publisher to use or reproduce any part of this book.

Contents

1. Faith Is Obedience and Obedience Is Faith...... 1
2. Faith Is Obeying The Gospel 4
3. Faith is Obedience in Little Things 6
4. Faith Is to Obey Pleasurable Commands 10
5. Faith Is To Go Forward 13
6. Faith is a Small Step of Obedience 15
7. Your Faith Is Your Life 18
8. Faith Is To Predict 20
9. Faith Is To Stagger Not 23
10. Your Faith Is Your Attitude 26
11. Faith Loves Preparation 29
12. Faith Is to Make Adjustments 31
13. Faith Is To Fight 33
14. Faith Is to Experience Painful Things for God 35
15. Faith Is to Lead with Strength 38
16. Faith Is to Act with Speed 41
17. Faith Is to Travel for God 43
18. By Faith, You Will Pass Your Tests 45
19. Every Bad Situation Is Reversible by Faith 48
20. Bad News Can Be Reversed by Faith 50
21. Faith Will Block Every Arrow Targeted at You 52
22. Faith Will Put Out Every Fire That Is Burning In Your Life 54

23.	Faith Will Shut The Mouths of All Lions in Your Life .. 58
24.	By Faith, You Will Emerge out of Your Weakness 61
25.	By Faith, You Will be Younger Than Your Age 64
26.	Every River Can Be Crossed By Faith............................ 66
27.	Faith Is Prayer and Prayer Is Faith 69
28.	Faith Will Make You Conquer Sin In Your Life 73
29.	Faith Will Make You Climb Every Wall 76
30.	Every Mountain In Your Life Can Be Flattened By Faith... 79
31.	Faith Will Make You Endure Affliction 82
32.	Faith Will Enable You to Abandon Wealthy Cities for Christ 84
33.	Faith Giants Are Created by Hearing 88
34.	Faith Giants Are Created by Seeing................................ 92
35.	Faith Giants Are Created By Meditation........................ 96
36.	Faith Can Stand Alone 99
37.	Faith Is an Unstoppable Force....................................... 103
38.	Faith Launches You into Miracle Ministry 106
39.	Faith Is A Force That Can Suspend the Laws of Nature... 109
40.	Faith Blocks Curses.. 112
41.	Faith Is A Force That Will Exempt You From Evil 114
42.	Faith Moves.. 117
43.	Faith Does Greater Works 120

44.	Faith Works Quickly	124
45.	Faith Will Empower You To Subdue Nations	128
46.	Faith Enables You to Overcome Superior Enemies	132
47.	Faith Overcomes Rejection	136
48.	Faith Will Turn Your Weaknesses into Strength	139
49.	Faith Is Operating with the Consciousness of the Invisible	143
50.	Faith Is Partnering with the Invisible to Accomplish the Impossible	146
51.	Faith is a Power that Converts Defeat to Victory	149
52.	Faith is a Power that Converts Sickness to Health	152
53.	Faith is a Power that Converts Barrenness into Fruitfulness	155
54.	Faith is a Power that Converts Failure into Success	158
55.	Faith Converts a Wicked Man into a Good Man	161
56.	Faith Converts You into a Hard Worker	164
57.	Faith is Precious	167
58.	Faith Grafts You In	171
59.	Faith Forces God's Hand to Perform Wonders	174
60.	Faith Saves You from Perishing	177
61.	Faith Is Your Only Way to Please God	179
62.	Faith Is a Powerful, Inexorable Creative Force	182
63.	Faith Accepts An Inheritance	185

64.	Faith Will Offer the Excellent Sacrifice	188
65.	Faith Loves Adventure	191
66.	Faith Says "Yes"	194
67.	Faith Has An Unlimited Capacity for Visions	197
68.	Faith Grows	200
69.	Faith is the Trigger for the Supernatural	203
70.	Faith Brings Glory into Your Life	207
71.	Faith Is the Pressure that You Apply	210
72.	Faith Is Not in a Hurry	213
73.	Faith Is a Mighty Weapon	216
74.	Faith is Mysterious in Its Working	219

CHAPTER 1

Faith Is Obedience and Obedience Is Faith

Are you a man of faith and power? Obeying God makes you a man of faith.

Faith is equated with obedience in the Bible. A man of faith is a man who walks in obedience. If you obey the call of God, you are a man of faith!

You cannot fulfil your ministry without walking by faith. To walk with God whom you cannot see, you must have a lot of faith. Faith is obedience and obedience is faith! Faith is equated with obedience. So who has faith? An obedient person has faith. Obeying God is the exercising of your faith. If you are obedient, you are a man of faith.

Christians must value the need to walk by faith and live by faith. Christians must value the need to walk by obedience and live by obedience! If you obey things that God tells you to do, then you are a man of faith.

You can see from the following examples that *obeying God makes you a man of faith.*

Faith Secrets

1. **The Israelites' obedience to the commandment would have been faith in action.**

   And at Taberah, and at Massah, and at Kibroth-hattaavah, ye provoked the Lord to wrath. Likewise when the Lord sent you from Kadesh-barnea, saying, Go up and possess the land which I have given you; then ye rebelled against the commandment of the Lord your God, and ye BELIEVED him not, nor HEARKENED to his voice.

   Deuteronomy 9:22-23

2. **When you do not believe, you are disobedient.**

   Unto you therefore which BELIEVE he is precious: but unto them which be DISOBEDIENT, the stone which the builders disallowed, the same is made the head of the corner, And a stone of stumbling, and a rock of offence, even to them which stumble at the word, being disobedient: whereunto also they were appointed.

   1 Peter 2:7-8

3. **When you are walking in faith, you obey what you are told.**

   BY FAITH ABRAHAM, when he was called to go out into a place which he should after receive for an inheritance, OBEYED; and he went out, not knowing whither he went. By faith he sojourned in the land of promise, as in a strange country, dwelling in tabernacles with Isaac and Jacob, the heirs with him of the same promise:

   Hebrews 11:8-9

4. **Not obeying and not trusting are one and the same thing.**

   Woe to her that is filthy and polluted, to the oppressing city! SHE OBEYED NOT THE VOICE; she received not correction; SHE TRUSTED NOT in the Lord; she drew not near to her God.

   Zephaniah 3:1-2

Keep walking in obedience! Obedience is faith in action! Through faith your life will soon be compared to Abraham's. You will have a great ministry. By faith, you are crossing every wall, every river and every blockade. Keep listening to messages! It is your master key to increasing your faith. The more preaching you listen to, the more obedient you will become. It is not only when you listen to preaching on the topic of faith that your faith increases. All kinds of preaching increase your faith. Faith comes by hearing and hearing comes by the word of God. I see you rising and jumping into your new and blessed life of obedience!

CHAPTER 2

Faith Is Obeying The Gospel

Don't say you believe something when you don't obey it! All through the Bible believing is equated with obeying!

The gospel of Jesus Christ must be believed. The gospel of Jesus Christ must be obeyed! We must believe in Jesus Christ as the Saviour of the world. Although the gospel is an invitation to *believe* in Jesus, it is also a command to *obey* Jesus. To *believe* in the gospel is to pledge yourself to *obey* the commandments of God.

When you receive the gospel it is not just to give a mental assent to the existence of Jesus Christ. Believing the gospel is to obey the gospel of Jesus Christ. Notice that the scriptures below teach us that receiving and believing in the gospel is the same as obeying the gospel. All through the Bible *believing* is equated with *obeying*!

Faith Is Obeying The Gospel

1. Believing in the gospel is seen as obeying the gospel.

   For the time is come that judgment must begin at the house of God: and if it first begin at us, what shall the end be of them that OBEY NOT THE GOSPEL OF GOD?

   1 Peter 4:17

2. Believing in the gospel and obeying the gospel is one and the same thing.

   And to you who are troubled rest with us, when the Lord Jesus shall be revealed from heaven with his mighty angels, In flaming fire taking vengeance on them that know not God, and THAT OBEY NOT THE GOSPEL of our Lord Jesus Christ: Who shall be punished with everlasting destruction from the presence of the Lord, and from the glory of his power;

   2 Thessalonians 1:7-9

3. Obeying the gospel is all that God expects from us.

   But they have NOT ALL OBEYED THE GOSPEL. For Esaias saith, Lord, who hath believed our report? So then faith cometh by hearing, and hearing by the word of God.

   Romans 10:16-17

CHAPTER 3

Faith is Obedience in Little Things

And when the prophet that brought him back from the way heard thereof, he said, It is the man of God, who was disobedient unto the word of the Lord: therefore the Lord hath delivered him unto the lion, which hath torn him, and slain him, according to the word of the Lord, which he spake unto him.

1 Kings 13:26

Are you a man of faith? Yes! You are a man of faith if you are obedient in little things.

Faith is obedience and obedience is faith! Having faith in God concerning big things is as important as having faith in God concerning little things. Therefore, obeying God in little things is as important as obeying God in big things. Obeying God in little things is very important for your ministry. Most people are concerned about obeying God in the big things. But the little things are equally important!

If you have faith, you must have faith in the big commandments as well as in the seemingly little instructions. The story of the prophet who disobeyed the Lord will always stand out as an example of obeying God in little things and big things.

The prophet had such great faith in the commandment of the Lord to prophesy against the King Jeroboam. He risked his life in order to give this great prophecy. But he was also given a small instruction about his dinner: "Do not have dinner in the city of Bethel. Eat your dinner outside the city of Bethel." This was a far easier, apparently minor instruction. The prophet obeyed the big instruction but failed to obey the minor commandment of the Lord. Thus he made a big mistake in his ministry. He had faith for big commands but no faith for little instructions.

Many times I have seen pastors failing in ministry because their faith is only in the big instructions. If you tell them to pray, to fast or to have an all-night, they are likely to obey. If you tell them to communicate whilst on the mission, they are likely to disobey. I have seen people lose their ministry because they failed to communicate or stay in touch. The successful missionaries that I have sent succeeded because they followed the little instructions.

I have had the privilege of going to Korea to learn about church growth from David Yonggi Cho. I went to Korea to learn the big skill called "Church Growth". This was my whole intention. However, God showed me so many little things that were equally important. The many little things I learnt from Yonggi Cho probably outweigh the lessons about church growth that I received from Yonggi Cho. God showed these little things to me and they have radically transformed my life and ministry. I am sure you would like me to say what those many little things are but I will not say so here. Just believe that having faith, being obedient in little things may change your life even more than your obedience of the big things.

> And, behold, there came a man of God out of Judah by the word of the Lord unto Bethel: and Jeroboam stood by the altar to burn incense. And he cried against the altar in the word of the Lord, and said, O altar, altar, thus saith the Lord; Behold, a child shall be born unto the house of David, Josiah by name; and upon thee shall he offer the priests of the high places that burn incense upon thee, and men's bones shall be burnt upon thee. And he gave a sign the same day, saying, this is the sign which the Lord hath spoken; Behold, the altar shall be rent, and the ashes that are upon it shall be poured out. And it came to pass, when king Jeroboam heard the saying of the man of God, which had cried against the altar in Bethel, that he put forth his hand from the altar, saying, Lay hold on him. And his hand, which he put forth against him, dried up, so that he could not pull it in again to him. The altar also was rent, and the ashes poured out from the altar, according to the sign which the man of God had given by the word of the Lord. And the king answered and said unto the man of God, Intreat now the face of the Lord thy God, and pray for me, that my hand may be restored me again. And the man of God besought the Lord, and the king's hand was restored him again, and became as it was before. And the king said unto the man of God, Come home with me, and refresh thyself, and I will give thee a reward. And the man of God said unto the king, If thou wilt give me half thine house, I will not go in with thee, neither will I eat bread nor drink water in this place: For so was it charged me by the word of the Lord, saying, Eat no bread, nor drink

water, nor turn again by the same way that thou camest. So he went another way, and returned not by the way that he came to Bethel.

1 Kings 13:1-10

Through obedience in little things you will have a great life and a powerful ministry. You are crossing every hidden blockade.

Keep listening to messages! It is your master key to increasing your faith. The more preaching you listen to, the more your life is changing. It is not only when you listen to preaching on the topic of faith that your faith increases. All kinds of preaching will increase your faith. Faith comes by hearing and hearing comes by the word of God. I see you rising and jumping into your new and blessed life by faith.

CHAPTER 4

Faith Is to Obey Pleasurable Commands

Now Abraham and Sarah were old and well stricken in age; and it ceased to be with Sarah after the manner of women. Therefore Sarah laughed within herself, saying, AFTER I AM WAXED OLD SHALL I HAVE PLEASURE, MY LORD BEING OLD ALSO? And the Lord said unto Abraham, Wherefore did Sarah laugh, saying, Shall I of a surety bear a child, which am old? Is any thing too hard for the Lord? At the time appointed I will return unto thee, according to the time of life, and Sarah shall have a son. Then Sarah denied, saying, I laughed not; for she was afraid. And he said, Nay; but thou didst laugh.

Genesis 18:11-15

Faith Is to Obey Pleasurable Commands

Faith is obedience and obedience is faith! To have faith is therefore to obey all the commands of God. One day, God will command you to do something pleasurable. It is your duty to obey Him in that as well.

Indeed, we all accept Abraham as the father of faith. His greatest act of faith was to obey a pleasurable command of God. Having sexual pleasure with his wife, Sarah, was the big step of faith that Abraham took in order to become the father of many nations. The Lord appeared to him and told him he was going to have a baby in a year's time. This baby was not going to be born of a virgin (without having sexual pleasure). This child was to be born by having pleasure with an old and menopausal woman. Both Abraham and Sarah knew what God's instruction meant. Sarah asked, "Shall I have pleasure after I am old?" Everyone knew that the word that had come from the Lord meant that they were supposed to get together and have pleasure.

Will you obey God when He tells you to do things that give you pleasure, rest, happiness and enjoyment? Most of us are suffering from over-righteousness and therefore cannot relax nor obey God when He gives us pleasurable commands. We will fast, we will pray, we will sacrifice and we will give money to the work of God. But most of us do not have faith to obey His pleasurable commands.

BE NOT RIGHTEOUS OVER MUCH; neither make thyself over wise: why shouldest thou destroy thyself?
           Ecclesiastes 7:16

Not obeying the pleasurable commands of God is a manifestation of over-righteousness. Over-righteousness, self-righteousness and unrighteous judgment are dangerous and deadly sins. Accept God's blessings and stop fighting God when He gives you the moments of pleasure, peace and joy.

Failing to obey the pleasurable commands of God can end your life prematurely. Many Christians are destroyed because they refuse to believe that God gives commands that are actually enjoyable.

Through your obedience to God's pleasurable commandments, you will have a great life. You are crossing every tradition and every limitation. Keep listening to messages! It is your master key to increasing your faith. The more preaching you listen to, the more your life is changing. It is not only when you listen to preaching on the topic of faith that your faith increases. Your ability to obey God's pleasurable commands will increase. All kinds of preaching increase your faith. Faith comes by hearing and hearing comes by the word of God. I see you rising and jumping into your new and blessed life of faith and obedience.

CHAPTER 5

Faith Is To Go Forward

And at Taberah, and at Massah, and at Kibroth-hattaavah, ye provoked the Lord to wrath. Likewise when the Lord sent you from Kadesh-barnea, saying, GO UP AND POSSESS THE LAND which I have given you; then ye rebelled against the commandment of the lord your god, AND YE BELIEVED HIM NOT, nor hearkened to his voice.

Deuteronomy 9:22-23

Faith Secrets

Are you a man of faith? Without faith you cannot please God. It is imperative that you walk by faith! It is imperative that you go forward, go up, and possess the land. That is faith! You must decide to keep moving forward and possess the land that God gives to you. Advancing is an act of faith.

Moving forward is to step into new things that God leads you to. There will be uncertainty! There will be risk! That is where faith comes in. Faith is to move forward into unchartered territory! Faith pleases God! Going forward into unknown realms pleases God!

If you are a man of faith you must move forward. When you move forward you are exercising faith. Faith is obedience to the commandment to go forward. When you move forward in your ministry, you are walking in faith and you are pleasing God. All forward movements in the ministry are the exercising of faith.

People who have stagnant ministries have stopped walking by faith! To move forward is to walk by faith. Every time you move forward there is uncertainty and you are not sure whether you will succeed or not. Walking in the uncertainty creates the risk that characterizes every step of faith. Do not be afraid to walk in risk and uncertainty. That is how to exercise your faith! That is how to please God! Moving forward pleases God. Move forward in your ministry. Move forward in your church.

What has God called you to do? There is a new land, a new dimension, a new project, a new vision and a new level that lies just ahead of you. By faith you will move forward into all these new things. Do not sit there in doubt and unbelief. It is time to be a man of faith. It is time to move forward.

CHAPTER 6

Faith is a Small Step of Obedience

Whom shall he teach knowledge? and whom shall he make to understand doctrine? them that are weaned from the milk, and drawn from the breasts. For precept must be upon precept, precept upon precept; line upon line, line upon line; HERE A LITTLE, AND THERE A LITTLE: For with stammering lips and another tongue will he speak to this people. To whom he said, this is the rest wherewith ye may cause the weary to rest; and this is the refreshing: yet they would not hear. But the word of the Lord was unto them precept upon precept, precept upon precept; line upon line, line upon line; HERE A LITTLE, AND THERE A LITTLE; that they might go, and fall backward, and be broken, and snared, and taken. Wherefore hear the word of the Lord, ye scornful men, that rule this people, which is in Jerusalem.

Isaiah 28:9-14

Faith Secrets

Are you a man of faith? Do not say that it is impossible to walk by faith. God has made it possible for you to walk by faith by creating a walk that involves many little steps. Faith is not the obeying of one huge near-impossible jump. Faith is rather the obedience of one small step. Think of all the heroes of faith God used. Most of them took one small step. His commandments are quite possible for you to obey because they are always one small step at a time.

> **By this we know that we love the children of God, when we love God, and keep his commandments. For this is the love of God, that we keep his commandments: and his commandments are not grievous.**
>
> **1 John 5:2-3**

God will not tell you to build a church with five thousand members as your first commission. He will probably tell you to witness, win souls, start a fellowship and learn how to preach. As you obey these little steps, He will lead you to your destiny. Perhaps you are called to have a worldwide ministry. That is wonderful. To have faith is to obey one small step at a time. A little here and a little there! As you read this book, there is one small step that God has for you. That small step is the act of faith that will change your life.

What did Rahab do to be called a hero of faith? Rahab, the harlot, gave her house to visitors. She provided the services of a harlot to Israeli spies. This was something she was used to doing. The only difference was to have had Israeli boys in her house for the night.

What did Abraham do to be included among the heroes of faith? He obeyed God and had sex with his aged wife. This is something he had been used to doing in his younger days.

What did Moses do to become a man of faith? He threw a stick down and it turned to a snake. I am sure he had thrown many sticks down before that time.

Faith is always a small step! What is the next small step for you? God wants you to do something and it will never be a big thing. It will be series of small steps. The next small step will take you higher than you imagined.

> **By this we know that we love the children of God, when we love God, and keep his commandments. For this is the love of God, that we keep his commandments: and his commandments are not grievous.**
>
> **1 John 5:2-3**

CHAPTER 7

Your Faith Is Your Life

Behold, his soul which is lifted up is not upright in him: but THE JUST SHALL LIVE BY HIS FAITH.

> Habakkuk 2:4

NOW THE JUST SHALL LIVE BY FAITH: but if any man draw back, my soul shall have no pleasure in him. But we are not of them who draw back unto perdition; but of them that believe to the saving of the soul.

> Hebrews 10:38-39

I am crucified with Christ: nevertheless I live; yet not I, but Christ liveth in me: and THE LIFE WHICH I NOW LIVE IN THE FLESH I LIVE BY THE FAITH of the Son of God, who loved me, and gave himself for me.

> Galatians 2:20

All through the Scripture it is clear that the life you live is the real revelation of your faith level. A person who throws himself into fulltime business and occasionally gives an offering is at a certain level of faith. Another person throws himself into fulltime business and regularly pays tithes reveals yet a higher level of faith.

Many people think that to have faith is simply to confess that they possess many earthly possessions. This is a warped and perverted understanding of what faith is. Faith is far more than your confession.

Faith is your life! The life you live is the faith you have! If you live your life out in full-time ministry it is because of the faith you have.

If you live your life out as a missionary in a foreign country, it is because of the faith you have. You believe that eternity will reward you far more than any temporary rewards on this earth.

If you live a life of doing earthly politics it is because of your faith in politics and human achievements. If you live your life out as a businessman, it is because of your faith in money and earthly achievements. Your life reveals your faith. Your life is an expression of your beliefs!

What you do with your life reveals what you really believe in. If you continue to quarrel and harbour grudges, it is because of your beliefs in the way to rectify things. Your ability to forgive and leave things to God reveals how much you believe in God and His Word. Your whole life is an expression of your faith in God. If you live your life singing secular music to secular audiences it is because of your beliefs. The life you live is an expression of your faith.

Your life is your faith! Your faith is your life!

As Apostle Paul said, "The life I now live, I live by the faith of the Son of God."

CHAPTER 8

Faith Is To Predict

(As it is written, I have made thee a father of many nations) before him whom he believed, even God, who quickeneth the dead, and calleth those things which be not as though they were.

Romans 4:17

Faith is to predict great things! Faith is to declare great things! Faith is to speak great words.

I once heard a pastor prophesying to his congregation. I thought to myself, "How can these things happen?" I thought to myself, "He's giving them false hopes." But I was wrong. The pastor was walking in faith and creating things in the spirit. Faith is to predict great things! Faith is to speak powerful things into existence! Faith is to speak the greatest and most amazing declarations over the people you are shepherding.

Faith is what you say. Faith is to speak what you believe is going to happen as though it has already happened. TO SPEAK NEGATIVELY IS TO SHOW YOUR LACK OF FAITH. Speak positively and call things that are non-existent into existence. The more you speak things of the future into existence by your bold declarations, the more you show yourself to be a man of faith.

Faith calls those things that are not as though they were. Faith speaks about the future and declares great things. It is time to declare great things so that you can walk in the faith that God walks in. Declaring your doubts about everything is not faith. Sharing your fears with everyone is not faith. Explaining why things will not work is not faith. Giving us your logical analysis is not faith.

It is time to predict great things! It is time to be a faith man! It is time to declare that a good thing is going to happen! It is time to declare those things that are not as though they are! Speak great things into existence! Speak nicely about your marriage. Speak good things about your associates. Say great things about your church! Say great things about your ministry! Say nice things about your children! What you say is what is going to happen by faith.

Faith is a very important thing. Keep building your faith. Your faith will really help you. Faith is your secret weapon. Faith comes by hearing. The more you listen to preaching, the more you hear the Word, and the more your faith is built up! Keep developing your faith by listening even more to preaching and teaching.

Through faith you will have an international ministry. You are crossing every wall, every barrier and every limitation. Keep listening to messages! It is your master key to increasing your faith. The more preaching you listen to, the more your life is changing. It is not only when you listen to preaching on the topic of faith that your faith increases. All kinds of preaching increase your faith. Faith comes by hearing and hearing comes by the word of God. Keep listening to powerful preaching messages.

CHAPTER 9

Faith Is To Stagger Not

He staggered not at the promise of God through unbelief; but was strong in faith, giving glory to God;

Romans 4:20

Faith Secrets

The Bible is full of many fantastic promises. If you read the book of Isaiah you will see beautiful promises of God for His people. Amazing predictions of largeness! Some of these promises are so amazing that you could easily dismiss them as fairy tales. In the book of Isaiah, he tells the barren to sing a song. He predicts amazing blessings for the desolate. Take a look at it for yourself.

> Sing, O barren, thou that didst not bear; break forth into singing, and cry aloud, thou that didst not travail with child: for more are the children of the desolate than the children of the married wife, saith the Lord.
>
> Enlarge the place of thy tent, and let them stretch forth the curtains of thine habitations: spare not, lengthen thy cords, and strengthen thy stakes; For thou shalt break forth on the right hand and on the left; and thy seed shall inherit the Gentiles, and make the desolate cities to be inhabited.
>
> Fear not; for thou shalt not be ashamed: neither be thou confounded; for thou shalt not be put to shame: for thou shalt forget the shame of thy youth, and shalt not remember the reproach of thy widowhood any more.
>
> For thy Maker is thine husband; the Lord of hosts is his name; and thy Redeemer the Holy One of Israel; The God of the whole earth shall he be called.
>
> Isaiah 54:1-5

Many stagger at the promises of God. They limp away in disbelief when God wants to bless them. Faith is your ability to not stagger: Faith is to not be destroyed by doubts.

Do not say negative things about the promises of God. Do not negate the glorious prophecies that are spoken over your life and ministry. Everyone who has a worldwide ministry today never expected a ministry beyond his neighbourhood. It is God's power that has made some people have a worldwide ministry.

Learn from Ezekiel. When God showed him that the dry bones would live, he gave a clever answer. He could have staggered at the promise of God. He could have rejected the promise of God as nonsense. Everyone knows that dry bones cannot live. Even recently buried bones cannot live. How much more dry bones! But Ezekiel did not stagger at the promise of God. He knew that God could do everything.

> And he said unto me, Son of man, CAN THESE BONES LIVE? AND I ANSWERED, O LORD GOD, THOU KNOWEST. Again he said unto me, Prophesy upon these bones, and say unto them, O ye dry bones, hear the word of the Lord. Thus saith the Lord God unto these bones; Behold, I will cause breath to enter into you, and ye shall live: And I will lay sinews upon you, and will bring up flesh upon you, and cover you with skin, and put breath in you, and ye shall live; and ye shall know that I am the Lord. So I prophesied as I was commanded: and as I prophesied, there was a noise, and behold a shaking, and the bones came together, bone to his bone.
>
> Ezekiel 37:3-7

All I have to say is "Don't stagger!" "Don't stagger!" "Don't stagger!" "Don't stagger!" Faith is a very important thing. Keep building your faith. Your faith will really help you.

Faith is your secret weapon. Faith comes by hearing. The more you listen to preaching, the more you hear the Word, the more your faith is built up! Keep developing your faith by listening even more to preaching and teaching. Don't stagger at the promises of God.

CHAPTER 10

Your Faith Is Your Attitude

Now Abraham and Sarah were old and well stricken in age; and it ceased to be with Sarah after the manner of women. Therefore Sarah laughed within herself, saying, After I am waxed old shall I have pleasure, my lord being old also? And the Lord said unto Abraham, Wherefore did Sarah laugh, saying, Shall I of a surety bear a child, which am old? Is any thing too hard for the Lord? At the time appointed I will return unto thee, according to the time of life, and Sarah shall have a son. Then Sarah denied, saying, I laughed not; for she was afraid. And he said, Nay; but thou didst laugh.

Genesis 18:11-15

Are you a man of faith? Yes, you are a man of faith when you have a good attitude. If you laugh and scorn at something, it shows your low level of respect for it. If you mock me, you do not respect me and you do not believe in me. If you sit up and honour me, it shows you believe that I am a man of God.

When Sara laughed at the word of God that came to her, it showed her lack of belief. God noticed her attitude when she was spoken to. Without faith you cannot please God! Without a good attitude you cannot please God!

Your faith is your attitude! To have a good attitude is to have faith. To have a bad attitude is to show a lack of faith. If you have a bad attitude towards me, you show that you do not believe that I am a great person. If you have a bad attitude towards me, you show that you do not believe that I am important. People have a good attitude towards those they think are important. People relax and develop a lackadaisical and even negative attitude towards those they have a low regard for. A moody person with a bad face will suddenly brighten up and look smart when she sees someone she fears or respects. Your attitude is a clear revelation of your faith and beliefs.

God is watching your attitude. God is watching you closely. He notices the expression on your face. He notices your attentiveness and alertness when He is speaking. He notices your "Amen"! He notices the loudness of your "Amen" and the fervency of your responses. He notices when you sleep in the midst of His amazing ancient words of power and revelation. Your attitude truly shows your faith.

Faith is a very important thing. Keep building your faith. Your faith will really help you. Faith is your secret weapon. Faith comes by hearing. The more you listen to preaching, the more you hear the Word, and the more your faith is built up! Keep developing your faith by listening even more to preaching and teaching.

Have a good attitude towards the Bible! Have a good attitude towards the preaching of the Word! Have a good attitude towards every word from the Holy Spirit! Do not scorn at God's calling for your life. Have faith in God! Without faith you cannot please God. To have faith in God means to have a good attitude.

CHAPTER 11

Faith Loves Preparation

By faith Noah, being warned of God of things not seen as yet, moved with fear, PREPARED AN ARK to the saving of his house; by the which he condemned the world, and became heir of the righteousness which is by faith.

Hebrews 11:7

Faith Secrets

Faith loves preparation! Men of faith are always preparing for something. Noah was preparing for a great flood whilst men without faith carried on eating, drinking, planting, building, marrying and giving in marriage. The big difference between men of faith and men without faith can be seen in what they prepare for.

Faith loves preparation! Victory loves preparation! Faith loves victory! Faith listens carefully to all warnings and prepares accordingly. Faith prepares for war! Faith prepares for possible mistakes. Faith prepares for battles. Faith prepares for the future.

Semper Paratus is a Latin phrase that means "always prepared". It is used as the official motto of the United States coastguard. It is their motto because it means they are always prepared for an emergency. They know and believe that there are always emergencies, storms and howling gales. No one needs a special prophecy to know that storms and such like events are on their way. Faith loves preparation and will always make itself ready for what it believes is coming.

Men without faith are men without preparation! What are you preparing for? Preparation shows your belief. Some people try to amass wealth on this earth, preparing for the seventy years that they are not even assured of. Why not prepare for the thousands of years that are coming in eternity? *Semper Paratus*: "Always prepared!" That should be the motto of a man of faith. Prepared for the future! Prepared for eternity! Prepared for judgment! Prepared to meet your God! Always prepared!

Therefore thus will I do unto thee, O Israel: and because I will do this unto thee,

PREPARE TO MEET THY GOD, O Israel.

Amos 4:12

CHAPTER 12

Faith Is to Make Adjustments

But MY COVENANT WILL I ESTABLISH WITH ISAAC, which Sarah shall bear unto thee at this set time in the next year.

Genesis 17:21

AND ABRAHAM GAVE ALL THAT HE HAD UNTO ISAAC. But unto the sons of the concubines, which Abraham had, Abraham gave gifts, and sent them away from Isaac his son, while he yet lived, eastward, unto the east country. And these are the days of the years of Abraham's life which he lived, an hundred threescore and fifteen years. Then Abraham gave up the ghost, and died in a good old age, an old man, and full of years; and was gathered to his people.

Genesis 25:5-8

Faith Secrets

Are you a man of faith and power? Well, your adjustments and your adaptation is your faith. Adjust your life and adapt everything to the word of God and you will be a man of faith.

Abraham adjusted his Will. Instead of being "fair" and giving equal portions to all his children, he made adjustments according to the promise he had received from God. He gave everything to Isaac but gave gifts to all his other children. Isaac was the special child according to the word of God. He never lived to see how special Isaac would be but he adjusted his Will and shared his property accordingly.

Your adjustment and your adaptation is your great act of faith. When God speaks, He expects you to adjust your life and prepare for it to happen. God told Abraham that He was going to do great things with Isaac. God told Abraham that Isaac was special. He told Abraham that even though He would bless his other children, Isaac was His chosen one.

Abraham adjusted and adapted to God's decision. He did not favour his daughters as some do in their Wills today. He did not favour his firstborn child as some people do. He did not favour his youngest child as some do today. Abraham gave everything he had to his second-born son. Since Isaac was the chosen one, he gave all that he had to Isaac. To fail to adjust and to adapt is to show your lack of faith.

Faith is a very important thing. Keep adjusting yourself to your beliefs. Your faith will really help you. Faith is your secret weapon. Faith comes by hearing. The more you listen to preaching, the more you hear the Word, the more your faith is built up! Keep developing your faith by listening even more to preaching and teaching. Adjust and adapt yourself to the word that God has spoken to you.

CHAPTER 13

Faith Is To Fight

Fight the good FIGHT OF FAITH, lay hold on eternal life, whereunto thou art also called, and hast professed a good profession before many witnesses.

1 Timothy 6:12

This charge I commit unto thee, son Timothy, according to the prophecies which went before on thee, that thou by them mightest war a good WARFARE; Holding faith, and a good conscience; which some having put away CONCERNING FAITH have made shipwreck:

1 Timothy 1:18-19

Your fight shows your faith! Faith is to fight! There is a fight of faith waiting for all of us. When you stop fighting, it means you have stopped having faith. Having faith is not just having a deep conviction about something. Having faith is not just making a series of positive confessions. Having faith is fighting for what you believe.

What has God told you that He is going to do? Keep fighting for the will of God to come to pass in your life. Faith is the life you live. We live by faith! What you do with your life is your faith. So, what you fight for shows what you believe in. Your fight shows your faith. If you fight for a political party to come into power, it shows your great faith in human beings and politics. If you fight for people to know about Jesus, it shows your great faith in Jesus Christ. If you fight for the church to be built, it shows your great faith in Jesus' command to us to build His church.

Your fight reveals your faith! It is time to show God that you believe in Him. You can do this by fighting for the righteous causes in the word of God.

I am engaged in a war so that I can build God's house. I believe in church planting and church growth. No matter how much the church backslides, I maintain my cause to build God's house and to establish His people. All my fights and battles have to do with my local church, the other churches, the buildings and the offices of the house of God. My fight reveals my faith.

Faith is a very important thing. Keep building your faith. Your faith will really help you. Your fight of faith is a secret weapon. Faith comes by hearing. The more you listen to preaching, the more you hear the Word, the more your faith is built up! Keep developing your faith by listening even more to preaching and teaching.

What do you fight for? Are you fighting to make more money? Are you fighting to build a company or a firm? Are you fighting to help one political faction stay in power? All that you fight for reveals your faith. When you fight for all these secular causes, it shows that your faith is more in human endeavour than in God's eternal plan. It is time to show your faith in God by fighting for God's kingdom. Become a man of faith!

CHAPTER 14

Faith Is to Experience Painful Things for God

This is my covenant, which ye shall keep, between me and you and thy seed after thee; every man child among you shall be circumcised. And ye shall circumcise the flesh of your foreskin; and it shall be a token of the covenant betwixt me and you. And he that is eight days old shall be circumcised among you, every man child in your generations, he that is born in the house, or bought with money of any stranger, which is not of thy seed. ...And Abraham took Ishmael his son, and all that were born in his house, and all that were bought with his money, every male among the men of Abraham's house; and circumcised the flesh of their foreskin in the selfsame day, as God had said unto him.

Genesis 17:10-12, 23

Faith Secrets

When you walk with God, He will ask you to do things that may be painful. He asked Abraham to circumcise himself and his whole family. The pain he experienced was private pain. To walk with God you must know pain! You will know pain if you are a man of faith. As a man of faith, you will know private suffering. It is part of the walk of faith.

Why is that?

Most of our world is in pain and difficulty. This world has fallen into the hands of satan. Satan is the god of this world and most people under his domain are in difficulty. Even in America, where you would think that people are having a good time, many people are suffering. I recently heard that 76% of Americans do not have a spare one thousand dollars to repair their cars if it got spoilt. That is a very high percentage of the people in the wealthiest country in the world. In America today, there are lots of unsolved murders, killings and terror attacks everywhere. If this is what is happening in the richest country in the world, how much more other nations where there is so much more difficulty? What I am trying to say is that there is pain and suffering in the world. The whole world lies in wickedness!

And we know that we are of God, and the whole world lieth in wickedness.

1 John 5:19

To have God's heart is to see the pain and understand the suffering in our world. Most people do not have it easy at all. God often allows His servants to experience some of that pain so that they are filled with compassion and understanding for the weaknesses and failings in the world. Hardly do you find anyone serving the Lord without pain.

Abraham was asked to circumcise himself without anaesthesia. This brought about indescribable pain (Genesis 17:10-12).

Joshua was asked to circumcise everyone in Israel with sharp knives. Remember there was no anaesthesia in those days and so it must have been a very painful experience for them.

At that time the Lord said unto Joshua, Make thee sharp knives, and circumcise again the children of Israel the second time. And Joshua made him sharp knives, and circumcised the children of Israel at the hill of the foreskins.

Joshua 5:2-3

Job was a man of faith. Job was a man who knew all about pain. Job said the days of man are few and full of trouble.

Man that is born of a woman is of few days, and full of trouble.

Job 14:1

Jacob was a man of faith. Jacob was a man who knew all about pain. Jacob lamented about his short life with many evil experiences.

And Jacob said unto Pharaoh, The days of the years of my pilgrimage are an hundred and thirty years: few and evil have the days of the years of my life been, and have not attained unto the days of the years of the life of my fathers in the days of their pilgrimage.

Genesis 47:9

Faith is a very important thing. Keep building your faith. Your faith will really help you. Faith will help you experience painful things for God. Faith comes by hearing. The more you listen to preaching, the more you hear the Word, the more your faith is built up! Keep developing your faith by listening even more to preaching and teaching.

CHAPTER 15

Faith Is to Lead with Strength

And Abraham took Ishmael his son, and all that were born in his house, and all that were bought with his money, every male among the men of Abraham's house; and circumcised the flesh of their foreskin in the selfsame day, as God had said unto him. And Abraham was ninety years old and nine, when he was circumcised in the flesh of his foreskin. And Ishmael his son was thirteen years old, when he was circumcised in the flesh of his foreskin.

Genesis 17:23-25

Your faith is your life! A life that demonstrates strong leadership is a life of faith. Strong leadership is only possible by men of faith. It takes faith to lead people to new places. Human beings are full of grumbling, murmuring and disputing. Without faith in God most people would shy away from leading and helping people.

Abraham had great faith and therefore was a great leader. He summoned the entire camp and described to them how their penises would need to be modified in order to please God. You can imagine how shocked the people were when Abraham unfolded his new vision to them. Only a strong leader could do this.

I have known pastors who felt that their churches should be a part of our denomination. Indeed, they felt that it was the will of God to belong to a family of churches rather than to be a single stand alone congregation. Some of these pastors led their churches to join the family and were happily integrated. I was amazed when they changed their minds midstream and pulled their churches out of the fellowship. I realized that they had come under pressure from their leaders and other prominent opinion leaders in their churches.

Perhaps the opinion leaders in these churches said, "Why should you join that denomination? We have our own vision! We also have a mandate from God! Every calling is different! We cannot be under that man! Our name must not disappear! They are trying to swallow us! Who do they think they are?" Perhaps the wives of these pastors also joined in to murmur against the decision of the senior pastor.

It is your faith in what God is telling you to do that enables you to lead people through painful or tortuous routes. Strong faith will cause you to stand up against any form of dissent within the ranks.

I know some pastors who admired my teachings and church management methods. They wanted to lead their churches in the same way and develop their ministries along the same line.

They, however, met a lot of resistance and were forced to go back to their old ways.

Without faith and a strong conviction, you cannot move forward and you cannot lead people through painful and difficult patches. To fail to line up those around you is a sign of a lack of faith. Your faith in God must be bigger than your faith in the negative people around. You must believe in the ability of God to promote you. You must believe in God's ability to make everything work out right. There will always be difficulties in every decision. I am sure some people may have died from infections and accidents during the circumcision. A strong man of faith will press on and do what he has been asked to do by the Lord. A strong man of faith is a strong leader!

CHAPTER 16

Faith Is to Act with Speed

And Abraham took Ishmael his son, and all that were born in his house, and all that were bought with his money, every male among the men of Abraham's house; and circumcised the flesh of their foreskin in the SELFSAME DAYs, as God had said unto him. And Abraham was ninety years old and nine, when he was circumcised in the flesh of his foreskin. And Ishmael his son was thirteen years old, when he was circumcised in the flesh of his foreskin.

Genesis 17:23-25

Faith Secrets

Abraham's faith was amazing. On the day he heard from God about circumcision, he got everyone around him circumcised. There was no one-week delay. There was nothing like doing it next week, next month or next year. Faithless people are always planning to do things next week, next month and next year. Men of faith do everything "now". Abraham did not need one week, one month or one year to get circumcised. He just did it right away.

Faith is to act with speed. Faith is to act quickly. Faith is to speedily implement the things that God speaks to you about. Abraham acted on the very day that God brought up the idea of circumcision. To act slowly and to implement slowly is the sign of a lack of faith in your life.

People jump into action when they have faith. A person may hear the word of God that says, "What is your life? It is a vapour that vanishes." This scripture basically means that your life is short and it will vanish very quickly. If you wait till you are on retirement before you decide to act on it, it means you did not believe that your life was a vapour. You believed that your life was something that would go on and on and on. That is why you waited until you were fifty years old before deciding to serve the Lord. Do you think God does not want young, juicy, energetic and intelligent people to work for Him? Certainly He does! You are the one who did not have enough faith that would make you act quickly.

Your quick response reveals your faith. Everything must be now! Everything must happen now if you really believe that it is true.

CHAPTER 17

Faith Is to Travel for God

Now the Lord had said unto Abram, GET THEE OUT OF THY COUNTRY, and from thy kindred, and from thy father's house, unto a land that I will shew thee: And I will make of thee a great nation, and I will bless thee, and make thy name great; and thou shalt be a blessing: And I will bless them that bless thee, and curse him that curseth thee: and in thee shall all families of the earth be blessed. So Abram departed, as the Lord had spoken unto him; and Lot went with him: and Abram was seventy and five years old when he departed out of Haran.

Genesis 12:1-4

Faith gets you up and moving. Abraham was turned into a traveller because of his belief in God. Travelling always involves challenges and risk. It is much easier to stay in one place, within your comfort zone.

Faith is obedience! Obedience is faith! To disobey the instruction to move is a great sign of a lack of faith in you.

When the western nations really believed in God, they travelled everywhere preaching the gospel of Jesus Christ. They travelled everywhere building churches and raising new Christians. There are Missions buildings in many remote parts of the world that testify to this fact. Some of the greatest missionaries came out of America and England. William Carey, the great missionary to India, was full of faith in the Great Commission. He left his homeland and travelled to India. He travelled on a six-month journey by ship to India.

Adoniram Judson, the great American missionary, travelled to Burma because of his great faith in God.

Today, many Christians do not believe in the Great Commission. Today, they rather believe in prosperity. Today, Christians largely believe that God will give them lots of money so they can live a good life.

According to one study, seventy-six per cent (76%) of all Christians know little or nothing about the Great Commission. Since people do not know about the Great Commission, what will make them travel to the ends of the earth? To have faith is to travel for God in obedience to His instructions. Without travelling, there is very little you can do for God.

CHAPTER 18

By Faith, You Will Pass Your Tests

And it came to pass after these things, that God did tempt Abraham, and said unto him, Abraham: and he said, Behold, here I am. And he said, Take now thy son, thine only son Isaac, whom thou lovest, and get thee into the land of Moriah; and offer him there for a burnt offering upon one of the mountains which I will tell thee of. And Abraham rose up early in the morning, and saddled his ass, and took two of his young men with him, and Isaac his son, and clave the wood for the burnt offering, and rose up, and went unto the place of which God had told him.

Genesis 22:1-3

Faith Secrets

A man of faith passes his exams! Passing your tests is a sign of your faith. Abraham was put through a test. He passed the test with flying colours. He passed his test because he believed in God. He believed that God was good. He believed that God would keep him. He believed that God would provide for him. Indeed, God provided a lamb just as he believed. God provided all that he needed on the mountain of sacrifice.

People cannot enter ministry because they do not have faith. They are not like Abraham. They do not believe that God is good and that God will provide. Perhaps you are not entering full-time ministry because you believe that God is a bad God. You think that God wants to destroy your life. You suspect that God wants to destroy your career. You think that God wants to take away your prosperity. But that is nonsense!

God does not call people to demote them. God does not call people to destroy them. Think correctly and have faith in God. If God is calling you, it is only to bless you and help you. If you are like Abraham, you will trust that God is good and that he will provide. If people had this Abrahamic faith there would be more intelligent, educated, qualified and successful people opting for full-time ministry. Unfortunately, many intelligent, educated and successful people think that God is trying to rob them of their earthly possessions.

People fail their examinations because they do not have faith. Often, they do not believe that the exam will come on. Often they do not believe that certain questions will be asked. They do not believe that they have to study that much! They do not believe that time is short!

A man of faith passes his exams! Passing your tests is a sign of your faith. A lack of faith is often the reason why people fail their tests and examinations. A child who is failing exams often lacks faith in the importance of examinations. It is when we grow up that we know the importance of schooling. When you are grown up, no one has to tell you that you have to pass your exams.

A man of faith will count it all joy when going through various trials and tribulations. Without faith, you cannot go through trials and tribulations with joy.

Trust in God and you will come out shining. Job went through trials and temptations but he never wavered in his faith in the goodness of God.

Faith is a very important thing. Keep building your faith. Your faith will really help you to pass all exams. Faith is your secret weapon. Faith comes by hearing. The more you listen to preaching, the more your faith is built up! Keep developing your faith by listening even more to preaching and teaching. You will pass all your tests by faith.

CHAPTER 19

Every Bad Situation Is Reversible by Faith

> Jesus therefore again groaning in himself cometh to the grave. It was a cave, and a stone lay upon it. Jesus said, Take ye away the stone. Martha, the sister of him that was dead, saith unto him, Lord, by this time he stinketh: for he hath been dead four days. Jesus saith unto her, SAID I NOT UNTO THEE, THAT, IF THOU WOULDEST BELIEVE, THOU SHOULDEST SEE THE GLORY OF GOD?
>
> John 11:38-40

Faith is your key to reversing the bad situations in your life. Jesus Christ showed us that every bad situation is reversible by faith. Today, you must believe that God can reverse every bad situation that has cropped up in your life.

Jesus Christ came to the home of Mary and Martha. A very bad situation had occurred. Their brother, Lazarus had died and been buried four days earlier. Jesus was not perturbed by this bad news. He knew that every bad situation could be reversed by faith in God. He said to Martha, "Did I not tell you that if you believed you would see my glory?"

In this life, you will encounter many different situations. Not all of them will be good. There will definitely be some bad situations. Remember always that every bad situation is reversible by faith.

It is true that Lazarus was in the grave. It is true that Lazarus had been buried for four days. It is true that his body was already decomposing and stinking in the heat underground. But Jesus declared that if Martha believed, she would see glory. Today I declare to you that you will see glory as you trust in God. Whatever seems to be a bad and negative situation will be reversed by the force of faith. You will see power! You will see honour! You will see glory through your faith in God and His Word.

Faith is very important for your life. Faith will reverse every bad situation. Keep stirring up your faith. Faith will really help you. Faith is your secret weapon! Faith comes by hearing and hearing comes by the word of God. The more you listen to preaching, the more you hear the Word and the more your faith is built up! As you do, you will be reversing all the works of the devil in your life. Keep developing your faith by listening even more to preaching and teaching. You will be amazed at the effect that faith has in your life.

CHAPTER 20

Bad News Can Be Reversed by Faith

WHILE HE YET SPAKE, THERE CAME FROM THE RULER OF THE SYNAGOGUE'S HOUSE CERTAIN WHICH SAID, THY DAUGHTER IS DEAD: why troublest thou the Master any further? As soon as Jesus heard the word that was spoken, he saith unto the ruler of the synagogue, be not afraid, only believe.

Mark 5:35-36

We will receive different kinds of news in our lives. Some of the news will be good news. Some will be bad. In times past, we would receive news through letters, messengers, telegrams or newspapers. Today, however, a large part of the news comes to us through our phones. Our Whatsapp messages, our texts and our calls are often the bearers of the news.

In Jesus' time, messengers came in with evil tidings from Jairus' house. "Your daughter is dead." No one would like to hear such news in his lifetime. That is the situation that Jesus found Himself in. He immediately intervened and told Jairus, "Fear not. Only believe." Only believe what? Believe in God! Believe in the goodness of God! Believe in the goodness of Jesus Christ! Believe in the power of God. Believe that all bad news can be reversed by faith.

Indeed, all bad news can be reversed by faith. You must believe that the evil news that you receive can and will turn around by having faith in God. I am not saying these things because I am super-human. I am not saying these things because I have some power to undo bad news. I am only declaring what I see in Jesus.

Rise up and declare that every bad news that you hear is reversible by faith. Your faith will give you the victory. Faith is the victory that overcomes the world. Through your faith in God I prophesy that the bad news that is hovering over your life is reversed in the name of Jesus. Amen!

Faith is very important for your life. Keep stirring up your faith. Faith will really help you. Faith is your secret weapon against bad news! Faith comes by hearing and hearing comes by the Word of God. The more you listen to preaching, the more your faith is built up! Keep developing your faith by listening even more to preaching and teaching. You will be amazed at the effect that faith has on your life.

CHAPTER 21

Faith Will Block Every Arrow Targeted at You

Above all, taking the shield of faith, wherewith ye shall be able to quench all the fiery darts of the wicked.

Ephesians 6:16

There is no doubt that the servant of God will be targeted and attacked by the enemy. The shield of faith is what will block every arrow that is targeted at you. Make no mistake; satan has targeted those who cause trouble for him. He is planning and scheming on how to attack you.

When you see that flaming arrow coming in your direction, do not be afraid. Faith will block that arrow that has been targeted at you. You can see how specific an attack is. An arrow is a personal attack meant for you. An arrow is not directed at a group. It is only you that the devil wants. This particular trouble has isolated you and challenged you personally.

The devil is a failure and a liar. Even though you feel isolated in this personalised custom-made attack that he sends to you, your faith will block the attack. I predict your victory! I predict the end of that attack! Your faith in God will turn the situation around.

Faith is a wonderful key that will change everything about your life. Keep stirring up your faith. Faith comes by hearing and hearing by the Word of God. The more you listen to preaching, the more your faith is built up! Keep developing your faith by listening even more to preaching and teaching. Many people will desire to have the faith that you have. Faith will change everything about your life!

CHAPTER 22

Faith Will Put Out Every Fire That Is Burning In Your Life

Who through faith subdued kingdoms, wrought righteousness, obtained promises, stopped the mouths of lions, QUENCHED THE VIOLENCE OF FIRE, escaped the edge of the sword, out of weakness were made strong, waxed valiant in fight, turned to flight the armies of the aliens.

Hebrews 11:33-34

Above all, taking the shield of faith, wherewith ye shall be able to quench all the FIERY DARTS OF THE WICKED.

Ephesians 6:16

And he commanded the most mighty men that were in his army to bind SHADRACH, MESHACH, AND ABED-NEGO, AND TO CAST THEM INTO THE BURNING FIERY FURNACE. Then these men were bound in their coats, their hosen, and their hats, and their other garments, and were cast into the midst of the burning fiery furnace. Therefore because the king's commandment was urgent, and the furnace exceeding hot, the flame of the fire slew those men that took up Shadrach, Meshach, and Abed-nego. And

Faith Will Put Out Every Fire That Is Burning In Your Life

these three men, Shadrach, Meshach, and Abed-nego, fell down bound into the midst of the burning fiery furnace. Then Nebuchadnezzar the king was astonied, and rose up in haste, and spake, and said unto his counsellors, did not we cast three men bound into the midst of the fire? They answered and said unto the king, True, O king. He answered and said, Lo, I see four men loose, walking in the midst of the fire, and they have no hurt; and the form of the fourth is like the Son of God.

Daniel 3:20-25

Faith Secrets

Faith in God will stop the violence of fire. Shadrach, Meshach and Abednego are the great example of people who went through the violence of fire. You are a modern day Shadrach, Meshach or Abednego. Today, we have the threat of the violence of fire in our modern lives. There are armed attacks everywhere in the world. From America to Afghanistan, you can expect there to be some violence of fire. There are armed robberies everywhere. There are innocent-looking people who are heavily armed and ready to kill. In the olden days, there were dangers from wild animals. Today, human beings are much more dangerous than wild animals.

By your faith, you will stop the violence of fire. By faith, your house will not burn or catch fire. By faith you will not die by the violence of gunfire. By faith, the violence of attacks of armed robbers and murderers will not work on you.

By faith Shadrach, Meshach and Abednego did not burn. Your skin will also not burn! By faith a bullet will not enter you! By faith the bullet will miss your heart and every vital structure in your body. By faith, terrorists will not find you! By faith, armed robbers will not enter your dwelling place! The eye of the evil one who seeks to destroy you will go blind before he gets to you. The plans to invade your house will fail!

By faith, the people who tried to kill Shadrach, Meshach and Abednego were burned themselves. I predict that the terrorists and armed robbers will burn and kill themselves before they get to you. By faith, every fire that starts in your house will be put out. By faith your property will not burn down.

By faith, Shadrach, Meshach and Abednego escaped the violence of burning by fire. By faith, they obtained the promises of God that God would deliver them. In the same way, God will deliver you!

By faith, you will escape every single attack! By faith, you will not die because you believe in God. By faith, every violent attack to remove you from this earth will not succeed. You are crossing seventy years with ease! You will live to see your children get married. You must believe the word of God if you want to live long and experience divine escapes.

Though a thousand fall by your side and ten thousand by your right side, you will always be the fortunate one who escapes the violence. By faith, may you be "unburnable" like Shadrach, Meshach and Abednego! May the fire that burns everyone be unable to burn you! May the violence that affects everyone be unable to touch you! May the gun that is pointed at you misfire into the air! May you be faster than your enemy! May you find a hiding place from the heat, the fire, the violence and the terror! By faith you are granted a divine escape from every demonic surprise.

Faith is what you need! Keep developing your faith. Faith will really help you. Faith is your secret weapon! Faith comes by hearing and hearing comes by the word of God. Keep developing your faith by listening even more to preaching and teaching. You are becoming even more resistant to the violence of fire.

CHAPTER 23

Faith Will Shut The Mouths of All Lions in Your Life

Who through faith subdued kingdoms, wrought righteousness, obtained promises, STOPPED THE MOUTHS OF LIONS, Quenched the violence of fire, escaped the edge of the sword, out of weakness were made strong, waxed valiant in fight, turned to flight the armies of the aliens.

Hebrews 11:33-34

By faith, Daniel escaped being eaten by lions. Through his faith, he stopped the mouth of lions. This is what is going to happen to you. Those who think you are doomed will be surprised to see you coming out untouched and unharmed.

By faith, you will emerge as a champion in your company, your business and your church. You will soon become a national hero. Just as Daniel was preferred, you will be preferred and chosen over and over again. Everyone in the country will soon know you for good reasons. Daniel was preferred! You will be preferred soon! Daniel prospered! You will prosper soon!

So this DANIEL PROSPERED in the reign of Darius, and in the reign of Cyrus the Persian.

Daniel 6:28

Then this DANIEL WAS PREFERRED above the presidents and princes, because an excellent spirit was in him; and the king thought to set him over the whole realm.

Daniel 6:3

Prosperity causes people to plot against you. Many people plotted against Daniel. They had meetings to discuss Daniel. They had meetings that excluded Daniel. They murmured and grumbled against him. He was rejected of men. He was an outcast.

Then the presidents and princes SOUGHT TO FIND OCCASION against Daniel concerning the kingdom; ...

Daniel 6:4

In the end, their hatred for Daniel boiled over and they threw him into the lions' den. By faith, none of the conspiracies of men were successful. The men who hated Daniel were even more wicked than the lions. Their mouths and their hearts conspired against Daniel in a vicious cycle of hatred and murder.

By faith, you will escape the conspiracies of men. Every meeting that has been held about you and against you will turn into confusion. Every decision that has been taken against you at a meeting that you were not present in, will not prevail. By faith, you will overturn, overcome and override malicious and malevolent decisions made against your life. Just as Daniel escaped the conspiracies, you will escape the ill-will of your colleagues and hypocritical friends.

The mouths of the lions are stopped right now by faith! By faith, you are escaping the enmity and hatred that has grown against you because you are preferred. May you always be preferred! May you have the upper hand when you are surrounded by lions! May hungry lions never destroy you, even in your most vulnerable state!

Faith is what you need to shut the mouths of lions around you! Keep developing your faith. Faith will really help you. Faith is your secret weapon! Faith comes by hearing and hearing comes by the word of God. The more you hear the Word the more your faith is built up!

Keep developing your faith by listening even more to preaching and teaching. You will escape all types of lions by your faith in God.

CHAPTER 24

By Faith, You Will Emerge out of Your Weakness

Who through faith subdued kingdoms, wrought righteousness, obtained promises, stopped the mouths of lions, Quenched the violence of fire, escaped the edge of the sword, OUT OF WEAKNESS WERE MADE STRONG, waxed valiant in fight, turned to flight the armies of the aliens.

Hebrews 11:33-34

Daniel, one of the heroes of faith, emerged out of his weakness and became a strong, prominent national hero. No one could have imagined that the mighty Daniel who was posing as a Prime Minister in different regimes was simply a castrated eunuch. I cannot imagine the day of Daniel's castration when his testicles were cut off with a hot sharp iron knife. You can imagine the bleeding and the pain as Daniel was converted into a weak impotent man without sexual urges or feelings.

From this low point of weakness, Daniel was made strong and emerged as a national hero and is remembered as a hero of faith. Many people today name their children after this man who emerged out of his weakness.

Most of us have some kind of weakness. Through faith, you will escape from the effects of your weaknesses. By faith, it will seem as though you have no weakness. Perhaps, you are sick with a chronic illness. By faith, your life will be like someone who has no illness. By faith, you will emerge out of your weakness. Perhaps, you take medicines or injections every day. God will strengthen you and help you to emerge out of your weakness. By faith, you will be so strong that people will pray to be like you. You will be surprised when people want to be like you. By faith, you will cross seventy with ease and attend the funerals of those who seem to be even more healthy than you.

You may be divorced through no fault of yours. You may despise yourself because of your divorce. I have some news for you. By faith, you will emerge out of that weakness! You are just like Daniel! You may see yourself as being incompetent, incapable and unqualified for ministry. Through that weakness, strength is coming into your life.

You may have the weakness of a terrible marriage. Out of that weakness you will emerge with strength. By faith, people will admire you and desire to be like you. By faith, people will describe you and your marriage as an ideal marriage and say that they want to be like you.

Faith is what you need! Keep developing your faith. Faith will really help you. Faith is your secret weapon! Faith comes by hearing and hearing comes by the word of God. The more you listen to preaching and the more you hear the Word, the more your faith is built up! Keep developing your faith by listening even more to preaching and teaching. You will emerge out of weakness by your faith in God.

CHAPTER 25

By Faith, You Will be Younger Than Your Age

And he said, I will certainly return unto thee according to the time of life; and, lo, Sarah thy wife shall have a son. And Sarah heard it in the tent door, which was behind him. NOW ABRAHAM AND SARAH WERE OLD AND WELL STRICKEN IN AGE; and it ceased to be with Sarah after the manner of women. Therefore Sarah laughed within herself, saying, after I am waxed old shall I have pleasure, my lord being old also?

Genesis 18:10-12

Young people are happy, excited and energetic. The older you get, the less happy, the less excited and the less energetic you are.

Faith will turn you into a young person. When Abraham was ninety-nine years old, God spoke to him about having children. He was surprised because he thought he had passed that stage of life. Abraham took the challenge and decided to become a man of faith. In choosing to walk by faith he became a younger man.

Every time I endeavour to obey God and walk by faith, I find myself becoming younger and walking with younger people. Indeed, fulfilling the Great Commission will make you a young person. When I chose to obey the Lord and have evangelistic crusades, I found myself at the beginning of a new career. I was forced to start all over again. I felt as though I was in my twenties, just beginning my ministry. When I had to start a church all over again, it was as though I was half my age.

I am sure Abraham felt young and jolly again as he approached his elderly, grey-haired wife. Sarah may have been a wizened old lady whose bodily juices were all drained from her being. She may have been a massive, fleshy, overweight madam who could hardly move around. There are no real pictures of Abraham and Sarah so we just have to imagine the different scenarios. Whatever the case, Abraham and Sarah were back to their youthful days because they were walking with God. This is what is going to happen to you. You will be a young person again because of your faith in God. Faith is obedience and obedience is faith!

By faith, you will be young again! By faith, you will be nice for a long time to come! By faith, your energy levels will rise again! By faith you will be fresh, exciting and enjoyable to be around. By faith, youthfulness is springing up in you like a fountain of joy.

Faith is what you need! Keep developing your faith and you will be a young person again. Faith will really help you. Faith is your secret weapon! Faith comes by hearing and hearing comes by the word of God. Keep developing your faith by listening even more to preaching and teaching. Through faith, you will escape all the ill effects of old age!

CHAPTER 26

Every River Can Be Crossed By Faith

By faith they passed through the Red sea as by dry land: which the Egyptians assaying to do were drowned.

Hebrews 11:29

Every River Can Be Crossed By Faith

The Red Sea speaks of the greatest obstacle, problem and difficulty of your life. In the journey from Egypt to Israel, the biggest obstacle, problem and challenge was the Red Sea.

The miracle of crossing the Red Sea shows the difference between those who had faith and those who did not have faith. Those who had faith crossed the Red Sea. Those who did not have faith were drowned in the Red Sea. It was not wisdom that made the difference between crossing and drowning. It was not technology that made the difference. It was not education that made the difference. It was not money or riches that made the difference. It was not their nationality that made the difference. Faith made the difference! Faith brought victory over the greatest obstacle and challenge of their lives.

Today, the greatest natural obstacles are always the rivers, the seas or the mountains. During the Second World War, the greatest obstacle to defeating Adolf Hitler was the English Channel. How to cross this large expanse of water with trucks, troops, tanks, food, fuel, guns and other heavy metal equipment was the challenge. Even when the British and American forces crossed the British channel, they were faced with a series of rivers that they had to cross. This delayed their advance by several months.

The Israelites were able to cross through the Red Sea because they had faith. Faith was the secret weapon that God gave His people. The Red Sea destroyed the Egyptians because they had no faith in the God of Israel. You will be able to do certain things because you have faith in God.

I predict that you are going to go through your Red Sea and come out smiling. Your faith is going to work! Because you believe in God, things are going to work out. Your faith in Jesus Christ is going to be your great advantage. Some trust in money. Some trust in chariots. Some trust in education. Some trust in their connections. But as you trust in God and exercise your faith, you will come out shining.

Some trust in chariots, and some in horses: but we will remember the name of the Lord our God.

Psalms 20:7

Keep developing your faith. Faith will really help you. Faith is your secret weapon! Faith comes by hearing and hearing comes by the word of God. The more you listen to preaching and the more you hear the word of God, the more your faith will be built up! Keep developing your faith by listening even more to preaching and teaching. Through faith, you will cross every river in your life.

CHAPTER 27

Faith Is Prayer and Prayer Is Faith

1. **GOD INTERPRETS YOUR PRAYERS AS ACTS OF FAITH.**

   And he spake a parable unto them to this end , that men ought always to pray, and not to faint; Saying, There was in a city a judge, which feared not God, neither regarded man: And there was a widow in that city; and she came unto him, saying, Avenge me of mine adversary. And he would not for a while: but afterward he said within himself, Though I fear not God, nor regard man; Yet because this widow troubleth me, I will avenge her, lest by her continual coming she weary me. And the Lord said, Hear what the unjust judge saith. And shall not God avenge his own elect, which cry day and night unto him, though he bear long with them? I tell you that he will avenge them speedily. Nevertheless when the Son of man cometh, shall he find faith on the earth?

   Luke 18:1-8

Faith Secrets

Your prayer time is the greatest expression of your faith in God. Faith is prayer and prayer is faith! Prayer is released through faith. Every time you pray, you show that you believe in God. You must understand how God interprets your times of prayer. Jesus taught us to pray in the passage above. Yet, at the end of His teaching, He asked if the Son of Man would find faith on the earth.

He did not ask if the Son of Man would find people praying because God interprets all your prayers as acts of faith. After all, it takes faith to stay in a room and talk to someone whom you cannot see. It takes faith to talk to someone for hours when he does not say a word back to you. *Your prayer time is the greatest expression of your faith in God.* Your ability to stay in one place and pray shows that you have faith in a real God.

2. GOD SEES YOUR PRAYERS AS FAITH.

And Jesus answering saith unto them, Have faith in God. For verily I say unto you, That whosoever shall say unto this mountain, Be thou removed, and be thou cast into the sea; and shall not doubt in his heart, but shall believe that those things which he saith shall come to pass; he shall have whatsoever he saith. Therefore I say unto you, What things soever ye desire, when ye pray, believe that ye receive them, and ye shall have them. And when ye stand praying, forgive, if ye have ought against any: that your Father also which is in heaven may forgive you your trespasses. But if ye do not forgive, neither will your Father which is in heaven forgive your trespasses.

Mark 11:22-26

The most famous teaching on faith is found in the eleventh chapter of Mark. In this famous teaching, Jesus taught; "Have faith in God." Jesus taught on how to move mountains and how to speak positive confessions.

Jesus also taught us to pray as an expression of our faith. Indeed, prayer is an expression of your faith in an invisible

God. Faith is prayer and prayer is faith! Every time you open your mouth to pray, you demonstrate that you have faith in God.

3. **GOD ACCEPTS YOUR PRAYERS AS FAITH.**

   So Jonah arose, and went unto Nineveh, according to the word of the Lord. Now Nineveh was an exceeding great city of three days' journey. And Jonah began to enter into the city a day's journey, and he cried, and said, yet forty days, and Nineveh shall be overthrown. SO THE PEOPLE OF NINEVEH BELIEVED GOD, AND PROCLAIMED A FAST, AND PUT ON SACKCLOTH, FROM THE GREATEST OF THEM EVEN TO THE LEAST OF THEM. For word came unto the king of Nineveh, and he arose from his throne, and he laid his robe from him, and covered him with sackcloth, and sat in ashes... Who can tell if God will turn and repent, and turn away from his fierce anger, that we perish not? And God saw their works, that they turned from their evil way; and God repented of the evil, that he had said that he would do unto them; and he did it not.

   Jonah 3:3-6, 9-10

   Faith is prayer and prayer is faith! The people of Nineveh proved that prayer is faith and faith is prayer. The account in Jonah shows how the people of Nineveh were turned to prayer and fasting because they believed the message from God. Their prayer and fasting was recognised as faith in God. This was a fast that even animals joined in. The greatest to the least in Nineveh went into prayer and fasting because they believed in God. The prayer of the people of Nineveh was the great act of faith God was looking for.

4. **GOD RECOGNIZES YOUR PRAYERS AS GREATER WORKS OF FAITH.**

   Verily, verily, I say unto you, HE THAT BELIEVETH ON ME, the works that I do shall he do also; and

greater works than these shall he do; because I go unto my Father. AND WHATSOEVER YE SHALL ASK IN MY NAME, THAT WILL I DO, that the Father may be glorified in the Son. If ye shall ask any thing in my name, I will do it.

John 14:12-14

God is expecting greater works from you. Jesus told us we would do greater works. How was He expecting us to do those greater works? Through prayer! He that believes on me will do greater works by asking and praying in the name of Jesus. Prayer is always seen as an act of faith.

Faith is prayer and prayer is faith! Keep developing your prayer life! Be a man of prayer and you will be a man of faith! Faith will really help you. Faith is your secret weapon! Faith comes by hearing and hearing comes by the word of God.

Keep developing your faith by listening even more to preaching and teaching. Be a man of prayer then you will be a man of faith. God always recognizes, interprets and accepts prayer as faith in Him.

Without faith you cannot please God. This means that every time you pray, you please God because you are demonstrating faith in the prayer. Faith pleases God and therefore prayer pleases God.

CHAPTER 28

Faith Will Make You Conquer Sin In Your Life

By faith Moses, when he was come to years, refused to be called the son of Pharaoh's daughter; CHOOSING RATHER TO SUFFER affliction with the people of God, than to enjoy THE PLEASURES OF SIN FOR A SEASON;

Hebrews 11:24-25

Faith Secrets

By faith Moses overcame his attraction to the pleasures of sin. He was able to turn away from the attractions and temptations of modern Egypt. He turned away and walked deep into the desert and lived the life of a nomad for forty years. Moses chose rather to suffer than to enjoy the pleasures of sin. A normal person will not choose to suffer. A normal person will rather choose to enjoy the pleasures of sin.

Today, many struggle with sin, temptation and immorality. Satan accuses and abuses us all the time because of our failings. We have no peace in our minds and our souls because we are constantly dirty in our own eyes. There is good news for you and me today. Faith is a master key to overcoming sin and moral weakness. Fornication, immorality, homosexuality and all other perversions can be overcome by faith.

Sin is an evil thing with a power behind it. Sin is an evil, mysterious mutation that has occurred in the natural race. It is neither natural nor easy to escape from its power. There is an evil spirit behind sin. That is why it is called the mystery of iniquity. Sin is indeed a mysterious thing drawing even the most spiritual down, if it can. This evil power draws men who do not want to sin. Many people simply give up, as they are overwhelmed with the power of iniquity. This is where faith comes in.

For THE MYSTERY OF INIQUITY doth already work: only he who now letteth will let, until he be taken out of the way.

2 Thessalonians 2:7

Moses did not just walk away from the pleasures of sin. Moses walked away from sin through the power of faith. Faith will make you conquer, defeat, and control every sin in your life. By the power of faith, you will choose to suffer for God. People will not believe that you are able to take such decisions.

Faith is a very important thing. Faith is something you must develop because it will help you overcome the power of sin and iniquity. Your faith will really help you to be a good Christian. Faith is your secret weapon.

Faith comes by hearing. The more you listen to preaching, the more you hear the Word and the more you will overcome sin. Keep developing your faith by listening even more to preaching and teaching. Listen to the messages! Listen to good Christian music and become a mighty man of faith.

I predict that all forms of sin, wickedness, stealing, sinful pleasures, pornography, adultery, fornication, jealousy, quarrelling, gossiping, drunkenness, drugs and addictions will be overcome by the power of faith in God. By faith, you will walk away from all addictions that threaten your Christianity.

CHAPTER 29

Faith Will Make You Climb Every Wall

By faith the walls of Jericho fell down, after they were compassed about seven days.

Hebrews 11:30

Faith Will Make You Climb Every Wall

Which wall is keeping you out? There are walls that keep us out of where we want to be. Everyone has a wall in his life. Many Africans have an invisible wall keeping them within their countries and out of Europe and America.

Joshua and Caleb desperately wanted to enter Jericho but there was a wall keeping them out. A very high wall indeed!

Where do you need to be and where do you need to go? Perhaps you need to enter a certain group from which you have been excluded. Perhaps your lack of education keeps you out.

Maybe there is an upper class of the society from which you are being excluded.

A wall has been raised and you have been excluded from certain meetings.

Maybe there is a "wall of language" that keeps you out of a certain nations.

Faith will cause you to climb every wall that keeps you out!

Your ministry will no longer be confined to certain neighbourhoods and communities. You will climb the wall that restricts you to your community.

It is very difficult to have an international ministry. Languages, culture, nationality, colour, governments and racism form huge barriers that keep your ministry out.

Many missionaries have struggled behind the walls of culture, language, nationality, colour and racism. These walls have kept them from reaching the harvest fields. Today, the walls are coming down in the name of Jesus! You will enter the cities of Jericho that God has destined for you. No city will be too strong for you! How will this be possible? Through faith!

Through faith you will have an international ministry. You are crossing every wall, every barrier and every limitation. Keep listening to messages! It is your master key to increasing your faith. The more preaching you listen to, the more your life is changing.

It is not only when you listen to preaching on the topic of faith that your faith increases. Listening to all kinds of preaching increase your faith. Faith comes by hearing and hearing comes by the word of God. I see you running over the wall and jumping into the city by faith. I see you jumping into your new house by faith!

CHAPTER 30

Every Mountain In Your Life Can Be Flattened By Faith

And Jesus answering saith unto them, Have faith in God. For verily I say unto you, That whosoever shall say unto this mountain, Be thou removed, and be thou cast into the sea; and shall not doubt in his heart, but shall believe that those things which he saith shall come to pass; he shall have whatsoever he saith. Therefore I say unto you, What things soever ye desire, when ye pray, believe that ye receive them, and ye shall have them. And when ye stand praying, forgive, if ye have ought against any: that your Father also which is in heaven may forgive you your trespasses.

Mark 11:22-25

Through faith, supernatural things will happen in your life. When you do not have faith, there are no supernatural events in your life. That is why faith is important. Faith introduces the supernatural into your life.

A mountain speaks of something that is humanly unmoveable and unchangeable.

A mountain speaks of something that is bigger, taller and mightier than you.

A mountain speaks of something that cannot be moved by human efforts. Human effort cannot remove a mountain. Only a supernatural or divine event can move the mountains around on our planet.

Whatever human efforts cannot accomplish, God can do in your life. Whatever you cannot accomplish with natural strength will be accomplished with supernatural strength. Supernatural strength will make a difference in your life.

Faith will flatten every mountain in your life.

Faith is a force that will shift the unmovable rocks and mountains of your life. Whatever is immovable around you will move very soon in the name of Jesus! Whatever is taunting you will move away by the force of faith.

I once met a man who was so resolute in his stance against our ministry. He organised the community against us. He organised demonstrations against the ministry. He brought in lawyers to fight against us. He sued my wife and I. He dragged us to court. He served injunctions on the ministry. He sent bailiffs to my office. He refused to negotiate with us. He would not listen to reason. Friends and pastors could not persuade him. Both lawyers and judges were perplexed at his behaviour. I thought to myself, "I have never met anyone like this". This man became a veritable unmoveable mountain in my life and ministry.

But through faith, the mountain that was unmoveable ended up moving. There is no way that I could have predicted how this mountain would move. God intervened and from one day to another, this man was no longer in my life.

Faith will move every mountain. Whatever looks unchangeable, inflexible and unvarying in your life will be forced to move by faith. Expect a victory soon! Your faith works! Your faith will work!

Through faith you will move every mountain. You are defeating every inflexible personality in your life. Keep listening to messages! It is your master key to increasing your faith. The more preaching you listen to, the more your life is changing. It is not only when you listen to preaching on the topic of faith that your faith increases. All kinds of teachings increase your faith. Faith comes by hearing and hearing comes by the word of God.

Supernatural power is released into your life when you walk by faith. The supernatural power will move the immoveable, inflexible and inalterable situations around you. Do not ask me how it will happen. Faith works! God moves when you believe His word. Faith is obedience and obedience is faith. Obey God and the mountain will move. That is how to walk by faith.

Faith is prayer and prayer is faith! Pray, and the mountain will move.

CHAPTER 31

Faith Will Make You Endure Affliction

By faith Moses, when he was come to years, refused to be called the son of Pharaoh's daughter; CHOOSING RATHER TO SUFFER AFFLICTION with the people of God, than to enjoy the pleasures of sin ...;

Hebrews 11:24-25

By faith, you will be able to endure afflictions God has chosen for you to experience. No one wants to be afflicted. But affliction is part of the call of God. You may try to shake it off but you cannot get away from the reality of suffering and affliction in Christianity.

Faith will make you endure every affliction and every difficulty God takes you through.

Moses was able to turn away from the pleasures of the cities of Egypt. By faith, he turned away from Pharaoh's palace. By faith, Moses was able to turn away from all the privileges in the Egyptian palace.

Today, many Christians cannot serve God nor work for Him. Most Christians can only sit in a church and hope for prosperity to rain on them by a miracle. Faithless Christians are powerless to put aside pleasures, privileges and wealth. Unlike Moses, they do not have faith in God. When you have faith, you can accept to suffer for God. How can that be? Faith makes you see eternity. Eternity and heaven cannot be seen with the natural eye. You need faith to envisage your eternal home. You need faith to see your rewards in eternity.

Earthly-minded faithless believers are not very useful to God. All they see is this world! I have another world in view! I see another world looming ahead. Faith will give you the strength to accept and endure difficulty for the sake of Christ.

Through faith you will endure every affliction, trial, test and temptation. You are overcoming all things through faith.

Keep listening to preaching messages! It is your master key to increasing your faith. The more preaching you listen to, the more faith you have. It is not only when you listen to teaching on the topic of faith that your faith increases. All kinds of teachings increase your faith.

Faith comes by hearing and hearing comes by the word of God. Your ability to endure afflictions and overcome temptations is rising as you listen to preaching and walk by it.

CHAPTER 32

Faith Will Enable You to Abandon Wealthy Cities for Christ

By faith he forsook Egypt, not fearing the wrath of the king: for he endured, as seeing him who is invisible.

Hebrews 11:27

Have faith in God and you will be able to go where God sends you. Most people are stuck in one place and unable to move to the place of their prosperity. Sometimes, it is where you are located that determines your prosperity; whether you will flourish or not.

Your master key to increasing your faith is in hearing a word from God. The more preaching you listen to, the more faith you will have. It is not only when you listen to teaching on the topic of faith that your faith increases. All kinds of teachings increase your faith. Faith comes by hearing and hearing comes by the word of God.

Moses had to migrate to the deserts and the wilderness in order to become the great prophet he was.

Joseph had to go to Egypt before he could become the famous Prime Minister and economic consultant that he was.

Ruth had to leave Moab and go to Israel in order to become the great grandmother of David.

Jesus had to go to Chorazin and Bethsaida in order to do His greatest works. He simply could not do great works in Nazareth and other places where He had grown up.

Today, there is a city, there is a community, there is a nation that awaits you. Without faith you will not go there. Without faith, you will not follow the leading of the Lord and head to the city of your destiny.

Many Christians follow money instead of following God. Many believers follow the bright flashing lights of wealthy cities instead of following God. When you are a man of faith, you will follow the word of God and believe in the Holy Spirit.

I remember a story I heard some years ago. There was a pastor who had a young beautiful daughter. One day, the daughter said she was tired of Christianity. She said, she was tired of going to church every day. She said she was tired of the Christian way of doing things. She wanted to find out for herself what the world had for her. She felt she was being deprived of the joys, excitement and pleasures of life.

Her parents were stunned by their daughter's speech. They felt it was wise to simply allow her to do whatever she wanted to do. But that night, she had a dream. In the dream, she was standing on the road side, in between two cities. One city had bright shining flashy lights that were very attractive. The other city was also lighted but was much dimmer and much less attractive.

Suddenly, a man appeared to her right hand side and said, "It seems you are interested in the brighter city. I can take you there. I know my way around." She was excited to meet this stranger who was a well-dressed and handsome gentleman. They entered the attractive city of bright, flashing and twirling lights and she was enthralled by the sights and sounds she encountered.

When they were deep in the city, she turned to look at the gentleman who was taking her round and his features had changed. His features were actually changing as she looked at him. He became more and more ugly until she realised that he was the devil himself. Suddenly, the lights in the bright and attractive city began to go off. In a few moments, she was terrified to find herself standing in the middle of a dark city with the devil himself as a companion. She screamed and woke up from her dream! The next day, she went back to her parents and told them, "Dear parents, I have changed my mind. I no longer want to find out what this world has for me. I want to stay in church and in Christ."

This story shows how Christians are following the deceptive and flashing attractions of this world. Moses was a man of faith. He turned away from Egypt and headed straight to the wilderness. His eyes were certainly not on the attractions of Egypt. He could see something that others could not see.

Faith will enable you abandon rich cities and important places for the sake of Christ. Do not follow a career in a place just because it is in a famous city. Your destiny may not be in New York, Paris, Brussels, Copenhagen, Los Angeles, London,

Tokyo, Kuala-Lumpur, Accra, Lagos or Johannesburg. Your destiny may be found in a small and unknown community where God would have you labour in His name.

Your ability to walk away from rich and affluent cities is rising as you listen to preaching. Your ability to walk away from wealthy cities is your ability to walk into your destiny. Keep listening to preaching messages! It is your master key to increasing your faith. The more preaching you listen to, the more faith you have. All kinds of teachings increase your faith. Faith comes by hearing and hearing comes by the word of God.

CHAPTER 33

Faith Giants Are Created by Hearing

So then faith cometh by hearing, and hearing by the word of God.

Romans 10:17

Faith is an unstoppable force and you need as much of it as you can get.

Faith rises and falls depending on the amount of hearing you do. The more you hear, the more the force of faith arises within you. God has given us a clear key to acquiring more of this unstoppable force. Hearing and hearing!

In today's world, it is even more possible to hear the word of God whenever you want to. You can play preaching and teaching all day long through your phone, through the internet, through your hard drives, through your car and much more. It is now *your* fault if you do not expose yourself to more and more preaching and teaching.

In 1988, as a medical student, I exposed myself to preaching by Kenneth Hagin. I loved listening to his teaching. I was drawn inexorably to his tapes and I put them on as my companions. My room was never quiet because his preaching would be heard night and day. I rarely pray in a silent room. The atmosphere is always regulated by the sound of preaching or singing. Whilst listening to Kenneth Hagin, I learnt about demons and how to deal with them. That is what he was preaching about when at a point, I felt God was telling me "From today you can teach." I believed it! I received a word from the Lord and I believed it! My whole life and ministry changed from that word that I believed.

Today, I am teaching the word of God to you through this book. How did I get here? I got here by hearing and hearing and hearing and hearing! Your ability to expose yourself to the hearing of the word of God is a master key to your spiritual development.

People often make the mistake of thinking that faith comes because you hear a message about faith. Faith is far bigger than being a topic in a list. Faith is your trust in God. The closer you are to God and the more real He is to you, the more you have faith in God. Any kind of preaching brings you close to God. Any kind of spiritual interaction makes you close to God. The closer you are to God and the more real He is to you, the more you believe in Him.

You must train yourself in the habit of listening to preaching. I can see ministers of the gospel who are so dry and lifeless because they do not expose themselves to the hearing of the word of God. This great habit of listening to the preaching will transform your very life. Faith giants are created by hearing!

What Do You Listen to?

Assemble for yourself a large collection of preaching materials. Allow the Holy Spirit to lead you to what you must listen to. You must always listen to people whom you believe are great. You must follow people who you genuinely think are great people. Notice what Jesus thought about John the Baptist. Jesus spoke about John the Baptist when his disciples were not there. This shows that he was speaking out of His genuine and heartfelt opinion. His heartfelt opinion of John the Baptist was that he was the greatest prophet ever. You must always listen to people you feel are really the greatest. Those are the people you must listen to.

> **And WHEN THE MESSENGERS OF JOHN WERE DEPARTED, HE BEGAN TO SPEAK unto the people concerning John, What went ye out into the wilderness for to see? A reed shaken with the wind? . ... For I say unto you, Among those that are born of women THERE IS NOT A GREATER prophet than John the Baptist: but he that is least in the kingdom of God is greater than he.**
>
> **Luke 7:24, 28**

When choosing whom to listen to, you must look for those who have the anointing remaining on their lives. Today, a lot of people claim to be anointed. You must look at those on whom the anointing has stayed for some years. John the Baptist was told whom to notice and whom to listen to. He was told to look out for someone on whom the anointing remained. There are many people who start out in the ministry but do not last. They seem to be anointed for a short while and cause a great stir.

But soon they are no more. Who do you know on whom the anointing has been sustained? Listen to those kinds of people.

> **And I knew him not: but he that sent me to baptize with water, the same said unto me, UPON WHOM THOU SHALT SEE THE SPIRIT DESCENDING, AND REMAINING on him, the same is he which baptizeth with the Holy Ghost.**
>
> **John 1:33**

CHAPTER 34

Faith Giants Are Created by Seeing

And as he talked with them, behold, there came up the champion, the Philistine of Gath, Goliath by name, out of the armies of the Philistines, and spake according to the same words: and David heard them. And all the men of Israel, WHEN THEY SAW THE MAN, FLED FROM HIM, AND WERE SORE AFRAID.

1 Samuel 17:23-24

And WHEN THE DISCIPLES SAW HIM WALKING ON THE SEA, THEY WERE TROUBLED, SAYING, IT IS A SPIRIT; AND THEY CRIED OUT FOR FEAR. But straightway Jesus spake unto them, saying, Be of good cheer; it is I; be not afraid. And Peter answered him and said, Lord, if it be thou, bid me come unto thee on the water. And he said, Come. And when Peter was come down out of the ship, he walked on the water, to go to Jesus. But when he saw the wind boisterous, he was afraid; and beginning to sink, he cried, saying, Lord, save me. And immediately Jesus stretched forth his hand, and caught him, and said unto him, O thou of little faith, wherefore didst thou doubt?

Matthew 14:26-31

Faith Giants Are Created by Seeing

Faith is an unstoppable force and you need as much of it as you can get.

Faith rises and falls depending on what you see. The more you see, the more the force of faith arises within you. God has given us a clear key to acquiring more of this unstoppable force. Seeing and seeing!

When the Israelites saw Goliath, they were filled with fear. Fear is a type of faith. It is negative faith. Fear is faith in things you do not want! Fear is a passionate, emotion-filled kind of faith. But it is faith in exactly what you hope will never happen.

What you see fills your soul with images that are difficult to shake off. Every image you picture in your soul is linked to other related images. As soon as you picture Goliath, you can picture his sword and you can imagine his brutality. Then you can imagine your head being chopped off. You then see pictures of your body lying on the left with your head rolling down the hill. You imagine your blood being spilled on the ground. All these images come from having set eyes on Goliath.

Fear is negative faith! When the disciples saw Jesus walking on the sea, they were filled with fear. They imagined ghosts coming from the underworld to capture them and carry them away. They imagined a string of ghoulish creatures from the dark underworld making their way to the boat to take them to hell. They panicked, and I am sure some of them wet themselves. When they calmed down, Peter was encouraged to come walk on the water. When he saw the boisterous wind, he was afraid and began to sink. The wind and the waves of the sea caused him to panic. He immediately pictured himself under the water and unable to breathe. He saw images of his body on the shore. He saw his funeral. He saw his wife weeping and the rest of his family mourning. He saw everyone sitting in black, looking at his drowned body. One picture sent him reeling. It is important that you know and understand the word of God if you really want to overcome the things you see.

Years ago I met a very beautiful girl. All girls are beautiful but some have a little something extra. This one had a little extra something. As the years passed by, I noticed that she was unable to enter a relationship, nor was she able to get married.

Was it that she was not getting suitors? Certainly not! Many young men wanted to marry her. Some were bankers, some were professionals and some were Christians. Indeed she had a large variety to choose from. But she wanted no one! The years went by. Then she turned twenty-five. Then thirty. Then she became forty years old. Then she became fifty. Then fifty-five. Still this girl wanted no one! I wondered why till I found out why.

She had lived with her father and mother happily, till her home was invaded by another woman. Her parents' marriage broke up and she watched her mother fall apart for many years.

This experience had a profound effect on her. What she saw in her home completely destroyed her soul, and she was filled with fear. Even when the best suitors proposed to her, she was unable to enter into a relationship. I am sure that every time a brother proposed to her, she had visions of her weeping, broken, disappointed, disillusioned and disheartened mother. Negative faith had overwhelmed her soul.

In your walk with God, there are certain things you need to see. There are certain things that will stay in you because you saw them. When you see the power of God it affects you even more than when you hear about it. When you see miracles, crusades and crowds, your faith is affected. Faith comes to you based on the things you see. Indeed, there is no clear scripture that says, "Faith comes by seeing" but there are a lot of scriptures that show us that faith does come to those who see certain things.

It is important that you watch videos of certain miracle services and crusades. There are certain things you can get by hearing. But there are certain things you can only get by seeing! Faith is an unstoppable force and it also comes by what you see.

Travel and see, as they say! Go to the places God directs you to. The more you see the things that others accomplish, the more you will have faith to do the same!

Most people build things they have seen! Most people minister like the people they have watched all their lives! Most people simply do what they have seen.

In the medical school, we were taught certain things in class. We were also told to "Watch one, assist one, then do one"! The higher skills of becoming a surgeon were only acquired by watching, assisting and then doing. Those high skills were not acquired by listening to lectures. You simply had to watch it being done. Then watch even more closely by assisting. After watching closely, you were qualified to do the same. You acquire faith and skills by watching. Faith comes to you through the things you see.

CHAPTER 35

Faith Giants Are Created By Meditation

Faith is an unstoppable force and you need as much of it as you can get.

Faith rises and falls depending on what you meditate on. You meditate on things you hear and see. The more you meditate, the more the force of faith arises within you. God has given you a clear key to acquiring more of this unstoppable force: Meditation!

Obedience is faith and faith is obedience. There is no faith without meditation. There is no obedience without meditation on the instructions you have received. Faith grows or diminishes depending on how much you meditate on God's word to you. You may be excited to hear a message from the Lord. You may even shout "Amen"! But unless you meditate on the Word, you will not develop the faith to obey it.

Faith is a type of obedience that is not possible without meditating on the Word. Joshua's only hope to prevent him from following the mistakes of his fathers was meditation. Notice the amazing faith blessings that come through meditation on the word of God.

1. **Faith for strength and courage for war come from meditation.**

Only be thou strong and very courageous, that thou mayest observe to do according to all the law, which Moses my servant commanded thee: turn not from it to the right hand or to the left, that thou mayest prosper whithersoever thou goest. This book of the law shall not depart out of thy mouth; but thou shalt meditate therein day and night, that thou mayest observe to do according to all that is written therein: for then thou shalt make thy way prosperous, and then thou shalt have good success. Have not I commanded thee? Be strong and of a good courage; be not afraid, neither be thou dismayed: for the Lord thy God is with thee whithersoever thou goest.

Joshua 1:7-9

2. **Faith to be happy and joyful comes by "eating" the word of God (meditation).**

Thy words were found, and I did eat them; and thy word was unto me the joy and rejoicing of mine heart: for I am called by thy name, O Lord God of hosts.

Jeremiah 15:16

3. **Faith for ministry comes by "eating" the books (meditation) God has given us.**

And the voice which I heard from heaven spake unto me again, and said, Go and take the little book which is open in the hand of the angel which standeth upon the sea and upon the earth. And I went unto the angel, and said unto him, Give me the little book. And he said unto me, Take it, and eat it up; and it shall make thy belly bitter, but it shall

Faith Secrets

be in thy mouth sweet as honey. And I took the little book out of the angel's hand, and ate it up; and it was in my mouth sweet as honey: and as soon as I had eaten it, my belly was bitter. And he said unto me, Thou must prophesy again before many peoples, and nations, and tongues, and kings.

Revelation 10:8-11

CHAPTER 36

Faith Can Stand Alone

Jesus answered them, do ye now believe? Behold, the hour cometh, yea, is now come, that ye shall be scattered, every man to his own, and shall leave me alone: and yet I am not alone, because the Father is with me.

John 16:31-32

Faith Secrets

Jesus believed in God. Whether human beings were with Him or not did not matter. What mattered was that God was with Him. Being alone was easy for Him.

Most people want to belong to a group. It takes faith to stand alone. Only men of faith do not need the comfort and reassurance that a group gives. Men of faith are ready to be alone! One time, Jesus asked His disciples whether they wanted to leave Him. He was ready to stand alone and have no disciples at all. Indeed, when He was arrested, all men forsook Him and He was left alone to deal with Pharisees, Sadducees, the Chief Priest and the Romans.

Most of the other heroes of faith were able to stand alone for what they believed. Do you have faith in God? If you have faith, you must be ready to stand alone for your convictions without any support from anyone.

People who always have to be in a group are not men of faith. If you cannot pray alone, you do not have faith in God. If you always have to be in a crowded prayer meeting, you are not a man of faith. If you have faith, you can stay alone for days as you fellowship with God and pray to Him.

Walking with God can be a lonely road. Your faith will cause a separation to occur. You will be rejected by men and despised by many because of your faith. Jesus endured the greatest loneliness because He was faithful to the Father.

When Jesus therefore perceived that they would come and take him by force, to make him a king, he departed again into a mountain himself alone.

John 6:15

1. Abraham stood alone. Abraham had faith to be separated from his family.

Hearken to me, ye that follow after righteousness, ye that seek the Lord: look unto the rock whence ye are hewn, and to the hole of the pit whence ye are digged. Look unto

Abraham your father, and unto Sarah that bare you: for I CALLED HIM ALONE, and blessed him, and increased him.

Isaiah 51:1-2

2. Jeremiah stood alone. Jeremiah had enough faith to be separated from his family.

Thy words were found, and I did eat them; and thy word was unto me the joy and rejoicing of mine heart: for I am called by thy name, O Lord God of hosts. I sat not in the assembly of the mockers, nor rejoiced; I SAT ALONE because of thy hand: for thou hast filled me with indignation.

Jeremiah 15:16-17

3. Jacob stood alone. Jacob was alone when he encountered God.

So went the present over before him: and himself lodged that night in the company. And he rose up that night, and took his two wives, and his two womenservants, and his eleven sons, and passed over the ford Jabbok. And he took them, and sent them over the brook, and sent over that he had. AND JACOB WAS LEFT ALONE; and there wrestled a man with him until the breaking of the day.

Genesis 32:21-24

4. David stood alone. David walked alone because he was anointed to be the future king.

Then came David to Nob to Ahimelech the priest: and Ahimelech was afraid at the meeting of David, and said unto him, WHY ART THOU ALONE, AND NO MAN WITH THEE? And David said unto Ahimelech the priest, The king hath commanded me a business, and hath said unto me, Let no man know any thing of the business whereabout I send thee, and what I have commanded thee: and I have appointed my servants to such and such a place.

Faith Secrets

Now therefore what is under thine hand? give me five loaves of bread in mine hand, or what there is present.

1 Samuel 21:1-3

5. The psalmist stood alone. The psalmist had faith to be alone with God.

I am like a pelican of the wilderness: I am like an owl of the desert. I watch, and AM AS A SPARROW ALONE UPON THE HOUSE TOP.

Psalms 102:6-7

CHAPTER 37

Faith Is an Unstoppable Force

And the Lord said, Simon, Simon, behold, Satan hath desired to have you, that he may sift you as wheat: But I have prayed for thee, THAT THY FAITH FAIL NOT: and when thou art converted, strengthen thy brethren.

Luke 22:31-32

Faith is an unstoppable dynamic potent force that stops all satanic attacks and onslaughts. Faith is an unstoppable, supernatural and invisible power. Faith is an active spiritual force that blocks ongoing attacks against you. It blocks the arrows of witches, the attacks of wizards and the attacks of demons.

Satan had planned to stop Simon in his ministry. Simon was under attack! Satan had planned to neutralise Simon and capture him. But Jesus prayed for Simon Peter that his faith would not fail. Faith was what would help Simon Peter overcome the devil.

When you have faith, you cannot be stopped. Jesus prayed for Simon so that his faith would not fail. Once Simon had faith, satan would not be able to stop him nor neutralise him.

Faith is the force that keeps you moving. Faith is the force that empowers you in the midst of your crises. Without faith, you will shrivel away. Without faith, you will buckle under pressure. Faith is a power that will work wonders in your life.

You will be unstoppable as Simon Peter was unstoppable! Faith is an unstoppable, dynamic, potent force that stops all satanic attacks and onslaughts. Faith is an unstoppable, supernatural and invisible power. Faith is an active spiritual force that blocks on-going attacks against you. It blocks the arrows of witches, the attacks of wizards and the attacks of demons.

By faith you cannot be stopped! You are defeating every wicked plan against your life. Keep listening to messages! It is your master key to increasing your faith. The more preaching you listen to, the more unstoppable you become. It is not only when you listen to preaching on the topic of faith that your faith increases. All kinds of teachings make you unstoppable. Faith comes by hearing and hearing comes by the word of God.

An unstoppable force is released into your life when you walk by faith. This unstoppable force will cause you to tread on scorpions and stamp on deadly enemies. Faith works! God will keep you on the move as you walk by faith.

Faith is obedience and obedience is faith. Obey God and you will be unstoppable. That is how to walk by faith. The demons will report that you were unstoppable.

CHAPTER 38

Faith Launches You into Miracle Ministry

He therefore that ministereth to you the Spirit, and **WORKETH MIRACLES** among you, doeth he it by the works of the law, or **BY THE HEARING OF FAITH?**

Galatians 3:5

Faith Launches You into Miracle Ministry

Faith is the key to miracles in your ministry! Miracles are worked out by faith. He that works miracles works them out by faith.

There is nothing like a miracle without faith. All those who experience miracles in their lives operate by faith. They believe in God and they trust God for His miracles.

Do you want to be a minister of miracles? Do you want to experience miracles? It is important that you operate in faith.

One day, I had a conversation with someone who ministered as a prophet. This prophet would publicly call out names, car numbers, addresses and other details of people's lives and give them amazing words of knowledge and direction. I wanted to know more about this kind of ministry.

He said something that struck me. He said to me, "Every one you see ministering and calling out names, car numbers, house numbers, passport numbers, etc., is exercising a lot of faith."

He continued, "I respect them because they are walking in great faith as they do these things."

I was taken aback. I asked, "Do they not see these details on a video screen?"

He said, "Not at all. They are ministering miraculous power by faith and they are always under a lot of pressure."

What this gentleman said to me confirmed what the word of God says. "He that ministers the spirit does it by faith". The scripture says clearly that those who minister the Spirit do so by the hearing of faith. Without faith, you cannot minister the gifts of the Spirit or anything to do with the Holy Spirit.

By faith you will become a miracle worker! You will minister with miracles, signs and wonders. Power will ooze out of your life and bless people but it will happen by faith. Keep watching videos! Keep listening to messages! It is your master key to increasing your faith. The more preaching you listen to, the more your ministry is changing into a miracle ministry. When you listen to preaching, your faith for the miracle ministry increases. All kinds of teachings will increase your faith in the miracle ministry. Faith comes by hearing and hearing comes by the word of God. As you walk by faith, you will minister the Spirit. You will minister in miracles and you will minister in power.

CHAPTER 39

Faith Is A Force That Can Suspend the Laws of Nature

And, behold, there arose A GREAT TEMPEST IN THE SEA, INSOMUCH THAT THE SHIP WAS COVERED WITH THE WAVES: but he was asleep. And his disciples came to him , and awoke him, saying, Lord, save us: we perish. And he saith unto them, Why are ye fearful, O YE OF LITTLE FAITH? Then he arose, and rebuked the winds and the sea; and there was a great calm.

Matthew 8:24-26

Between January and August 2017, seven people had drowned in the Sea of Galilee in just seven months, with dozens of others having to be rescued. Marine Police had warned about strong winds from the west which could carry swimmers away to deep waters. Indeed, even in these modern times, the Sea of Galilee is known to have four to five drowning accidents every year.

The Sea of Galilee is well-known for drowning accidents. Jesus would have died in the Sea of Galilee if He had not used His faith. He would have been drowned in that lake like many others already had. Jesus Christ suspended the laws of nature in the Sea of Galilee, which today drown four to five people every year.

Faith is a force that can suspend the laws of nature. This is why faith is important. Jesus suspended the laws of nature by His faith command. He suspended the storm and stopped the wind, the rain and the waves. Then He asked his frightened disciples where their faith was.

There are many laws of nature that you may have to suspend during your life on earth. By faith you will live longer than you would have lived. Nature, genetics and the environment may have determined that you should die by a certain age. But your faith can suspend the laws of nature. Through faith, you can postpone your death. That is exactly what Jesus did! Your faith will suspend the laws of nature. Your faith will postpone your death!

Nature may have determined that you should drown in a flood but faith can suspend the laws of nature for you. Faith can stop the swelling of a river and keep you alive. By faith, you will not drown.

Nature may determine that you should be buried in the next earthquake but your faith can suspend the laws of nature. Faith is an unstoppable force that can suspend the laws of nature.

Nature may determine that your car should skid off an icy slippery road. God's power can suspend the slippery nature of the ice. You may meet a hungry wolf-like dog in someone's house. Nature may determine that the dogs should attack you. By the power of faith, you will stop the attack.

This is why faith is so important. The laws of nature may not be in your favour so you need to walk by faith. Your genes may not predict a good outcome for your life. Have faith in God! Walk by faith! Keep watching videos! Keep listening to messages! It is your master key to increasing your faith. The more preaching you listen to, the more you will halt the forces of nature that are against your existence.

Many different types of preaching will increase your faith. Faith comes by hearing and hearing comes by the word of God. As you walk by faith, you will suspend all the laws of nature that are against your destiny.

CHAPTER 40

Faith Blocks Curses

So Jonah arose, and went unto Nineveh, according to the word of the Lord. Now Nineveh was an exceeding great city of three days' journey. And Jonah began to enter into the city a day's journey, and he cried, and said, yet forty days, and Nineveh shall be overthrown. SO THE PEOPLE OF NINEVEH BELIEVED GOD, and proclaimed a fast, and put on sackcloth, from the greatest of them even to the least of them. For word came unto the king of Nineveh, and he arose from his throne, and he laid his robe from him, and covered him with sackcloth, and sat in ashes... Who can tell if God will turn and repent, and turn away from his fierce anger, that we perish not? And God saw their works, that they turned from their evil way; and GOD REPENTED OF THE EVIL, that he had said that he would do unto them; and he did it not.

Jonah 3:3-6, 9-10

There are many curses and predictions of evil in this life. The reason for this is simple. We have so many sins, so many mistakes and so many weaknesses. All our sins are heaped up before the Lord and the curse is on its way.

The only way to explain life on this earth is to believe in the reality of curses. The Book of Revelation tells us that there will be no more curses in heaven. The one big thing that will be absent from heaven is the curse.

Faith will block the curse!

The people of Nineveh believed the message that was preached to them. Your faith will stop the approaching curse.

Your faith is blocking every curse spoken against your family!

Your faith is blocking every curse in your nation!

Your faith will block every curse that your parents have brought upon the family!

By faith, you will block every curse that you are invoking upon yourself!

By faith, every food you are given to eat will not make you sick!

The curse of the thief is blocked in your life!

There is no way to know all the curses that are operating against you. sThis is why faith is so important. Curses may have been spoken against you. You need to walk by faith. The curse is already in the atmosphere. Have faith in God! Walk by faith! Keep watching videos! Keep listening to messages! It is your master key to blocking curses. The more preaching you listen to, the more you block curses.

Many different types of preaching will increase your faith. Faith comes by hearing and hearing comes by the word of God. As you walk by faith, you will suspend all curses that are against your destiny.

CHAPTER 41

Faith Is A Force That Will Exempt You From Evil

Now faith is the substance of things hoped for, the evidence of things not seen. BY FAITH ENOCH WAS TRANSLATED THAT HE SHOULD NOT SEE DEATH; and was not found, because God had translated him: for before his translation he had this testimony, that he pleased God.

Hebrews 11:1, 5

Enoch was exempted from death. All human beings died but Enoch was exempted from death. Imagine that! Something that every single person goes through!

Faith is a powerful exemption force! Faith will exempt you from many evils! You will be exempted from many things because of your faith. As Enoch was exempted from death you are exempted from sickness, poverty, lack and want.

Expect to be exempted from evil! Expect to have a divine escape. Expect to come out alive by faith. By faith, Enoch was exempted from that which happens to everyone.

Everyone may fail his examination but you will pass in the name of Jesus.

Everyone in your country may be poor but you will be exempted in the name of Jesus. Everyone in your country may be poorly educated but you will be exempted in the name of Jesus.

Everyone in a car accident may be hurt but you will be exempted in the name of Jesus.

Everyone in a car accident may die but you will be exempted in the name of Jesus.

Everyone may fall asleep but you will be wide awake.

Everybody's child may not do well but your child will do well in the name of Jesus.

Everyone may be involved in fornication and adultery but you will be exempted in the name of Jesus.

Faith is important because of its power to have you exempted. A wide net may catch many people but you will come out having divinely escaped that which caught many others in an evil day.

A thousand may fall at your side but God is exempting you because you believe in Him. Believe in the prophecies. Believe in the unbelievable and you will have a better life.

Have faith in God! Walk by faith! Keep watching videos! Keep listening to messages! It is your master key to being exempted. The more preaching you listen to, the more your faith is built.

Many different types of preaching will increase your faith for exemption. Faith comes by hearing and hearing comes by the word of God. As you walk by faith, you will be exempted from the evil that comes to every normal person.

CHAPTER 42

Faith Moves

(For we walk by faith, not by sight:)

2 Corinthians 5:7

Through faith you will never be stagnant. Through faith you will never be stuck in the mud. God is on the move and those who believe in Him will have to walk in step with Him.

> **For in him we live, and move, and have our being; as certain also of your own poets have said, For we are also his offspring.**
>
> **Acts 17:28**

You must move forward and go further in God. Christianity requires basic movement. Christianity requires you to take steps. You will never take a step forward in God until you have faith.

Our most basic movement is to walk. Therefore, your most basic movement in Christ is walking by faith. The most basic moves you will ever make in God will require faith!

Since some people gave their lives to Christ, they have not moved a single step forward. There has been no advancement in God.

You have not left your old friends behind!

You have not broken out of addictions and bondages!

You have not left behind immorality!

You have not moved away from lying and stealing!

You have not moved away from laziness and fruitlessness! When are you going to take a step forward in God?

You need faith so that you can move forward. I see your life advancing in Christ.

That is why faith is important for you. There will be no forward movement in your life if you do not have faith. You need to move forward in your Christian faith.

Increase your faith in God so you can move! Walk by faith! Start watching anointed videos! Start listening to powerful messages of the Word! It is your master key to increasing your faith. The more preaching you listen to, the more your faith is built. The more faith you have, the more you will advance in God.

Many different types of preaching will increase your faith. Faith comes by hearing and hearing comes by the word of God. As you grow in faith, you will walk and advance towards God's destiny for your life.

In Heaven every step of faith you take is noticed.

A young lady died leaving behind her husband and one small child. The prophet had a vision and saw her in Heaven. By the time of this vision, the young man she left behind had remarried and moved on.

When the prophet spoke to the young lady in Heaven, she expressed concern about her child. She had not even noticed that her husband had remarried. She told the prophet, "Over here in Heaven, we see every step of faith you take". She had actually noticed when her husband was baptised in the Holy Spirit. She had noticed when he moved forward in God. But she had not noticed when he remarried.

This vision taught me that our spiritual steps are truly steps of faith. It is our spiritual steps of faith towards God's destiny that are important. It is time for you to move on in God.

To move forward in the Spirit requires faith. To hear the call of God requires faith. To obey the call of God and step into ministry is a wonderful step forward.

CHAPTER 43

Faith Does Greater Works

Verily, verily, I say unto you, HE THAT BELIEVETH on me, the works that I do shall he do also; and GREATER WORKS than these shall he do; because I go unto my Father.

John 14:12

Faith Does Greater Works

The works of Jesus were preaching, teaching and healing. To walk by faith is to do greater works than these! If you are not doing these greater works, you are not walking by faith. Why are you not preaching? Why are you not teaching? Why are you not healing? Why are you not a missionary?

Have faith in God and you will do greater works than your fathers. If you walk by faith, you will end up doing more than your fathers. Jesus clearly taught that walking by faith is to do greater works. He that believeth on me shall do greater works!

Faith is not about money, cars and prosperity. Faith is about doing greater works. Faith is to go preaching "into all the world". Faith is to go even further than your Lord Jesus.

For a certain woman, whose young daughter had an unclean spirit, heard of him, and came and fell at his feet: The woman was a Greek, a Syrophenician by nation; and she besought him that he would cast forth the devil out of her daughter. But Jesus said unto her, Let the children first be filled: for it is not meet to take the children's bread, and to cast it unto the dogs. And she answered and said unto him, Yes, Lord: yet the dogs under the table eat of the children's crumbs.

Mark 7:25-28

Jesus went only to the lost sheep of Israel. Jesus did not go into all the world. He resisted the idea of preaching to non-Jews. He really did not want to minister to anyone who was not a Jew. He told the Syrophenician woman that it was not right to give the children's food to dogs. The Syrophenician woman understood that she was the dog in the parable.

Jesus was not interested in healing Syrophenician people. But he told us to go the ends of the world, including Syrophenicians. Without faith you will not go to the ends of the world.

And there were certain Greeks among them that came up to worship at the feast: The same came therefore to Philip, which was of Bethsaida of Galilee, and desired him, saying, Sir, we would see Jesus. Philip cometh and telleth

Faith Secrets

> Andrew: and again Andrew and Philip tell Jesus. And Jesus answered them, saying, The hour is come, that the Son of man should be glorified. Verily, verily, I say unto you, Except a corn of wheat fall into the ground and die, it abideth alone: but if it die, it bringeth forth much fruit.
>
> John 12:20-24

Once, Jesus was told about some Greeks who wanted to see him. His response to that was to speak about the cross. Indeed, Jesus was highly uninterested in going beyond Israel in His ministry.

Jesus could have gone to India because it is a well-known fact that His disciple Thomas went to India to preach the word of God. Jesus Christ ended His ministry in Jerusalem. Then He told us to do greater works by going to the ends of the world.

If you have faith, you will do the greater works Jesus sent you to do. Without faith you will never obey the Great Commission.

Jesus was not interested in preaching to Greeks. Jesus told us to go to the whole world, to preach to every creature. Without faith you will not preach to all creatures.

> And he said unto them, Go ye into all the world, and preach the gospel to every creature. He that believeth and is baptized shall be saved; but he that believeth not shall be damned. And these signs shall follow them that believe; In my name shall they cast out devils; they shall speak with new tongues;
>
> Mark 16:15-17

Jesus told us to go into the world. Jesus Himself never went to the whole world. Without faith you will not go to the world. Faith is obedience and obedience is faith.

> And when I saw him, I fell at his feet as dead. And he laid his right hand upon me, saying unto me, Fear not; I am the first and the last: I am he that liveth, and was dead; and, behold, I am alive for evermore, Amen; and have the keys of hell and of death. Write the things which thou hast

seen, and the things which are, and the things which shall be hereafter;

Revelation 1:17-19

Jesus never wrote a book but He told his disciples to write books. Without faith you cannot obey this command.

This is why faith is so important. Greater works are only possible if you believe the command to go. Instead of doubting whether you have the abilities, you must walk on in faith and trust God. As you step out in faith, you will find yourself doing greater works than your fathers. Have faith in God! Walk by faith! Watch as many preaching videos as you can! Keep listening to messages in the house, whilst you are walking and in the car! It is your master key to doing greater works. He that believeth shall do greater works. The more preaching you listen to, the more likely you are to do greater works.

When you hear preaching on the Great Commission, your faith to go into all the world will rise. If you just hear preaching on prosperity and long life, you may not have faith to go into all the world. Faith comes by hearing and hearing comes by the word of God. As you listen to sermons on the Great Commission, you will find yourself doing greater works. Greater works are the portion of those who have faith. Greater works are not establishing secular institutions and creating wealth for Christians. Greater works are doing the works of Jesus.

CHAPTER 44

Faith Works Quickly

How long wilt thou forget me, O Lord? For ever? How long wilt thou hide thy face from me?

                                                                          Psalms 13:1

Faith works all the time! Our human instincts make us ask God how long it is going to take before our faith works. The answer is found in the word of God. Faith works within minutes, within hours, within days, within months and within years. There is no fixed formula for when faith works. Faith works as soon as it is necessary. God is not a computer. You cannot program Him to follow your schedule. If God answered prayer in a repetitive automated way, then we would not need Him. We would need a computer with intelligent software that is programmed to spew out answers to requests. God is far more than a computer.

1. **Faith works within minutes!** Expect healings to take place within minutes. Peter's mother was healed within minutes.

    And he arose out of the synagogue, and entered into Simon's house. And Simon's wife's mother was taken with a great fever; and they besought him for her. And he stood over her, and rebuked the fever; and IT LEFT HER: AND IMMEDIATELY SHE AROSE AND MINISTERED UNTO THEM.

    Luke 4:38-39

2. **Faith works in three months!** Expect a new level of glory and prosperity within the next three months. The glory of God working in Obededom's life caused a major change within three months. If he had rejected God's ark after one week, he would have missed the blessing.

    And the ark of God remained with the family of Obededom in his house THREE MONTHS. And the Lord blessed the house of Obededom, and all that he had.

    1 Chronicles 13:14

3. **Faith works within a year: Your level can change within the year.** The scripture below shows us how the owner of the vineyard expected a change in the vineyard within a year. Next year by this time your level would have changed. As you walk in obedience, your church is going to grow dramatically within a year.

Faith Secrets

He spake also this parable; A certain man had a fig tree planted in his vineyard; and he came and sought fruit thereon, and found none. Then said he unto the dresser of his vineyard, Behold, these three years I come seeking fruit on this fig tree, and find none: cut it down; why cumbereth it the ground? And he answering said unto him, LORD, LET IT ALONE THIS YEAR ALSO, till I shall dig about it, and dung it: And if it bear fruit, well: and if not, then after that thou shalt cut it down.

Luke 13:6-9

4. **Faith works in five years: In some situations, faith works by the fifth year.**

And when ye shall come into the land, and shall have planted all manner of trees for food, then ye shall count the fruit thereof as uncircumcised: three years shall it be as uncircumcised unto you: it shall not be eaten of. But in the fourth year all the fruit thereof shall be holy to praise the Lord withal. AND IN THE FIFTH YEAR shall ye eat of the fruit thereof, that it may yield unto you the increase thereof: I am the Lord your God.

Leviticus 19:23-25

Sometimes, faith works like the Chinese bamboo. Farmers of Chinese bamboo have their faith rewarded in five years. For five years there is no sign that their faith will be blessed. In the fifth year, the miracle begins.

The growth of the Chinese bamboo requires nurturing through water, fertile soil and sunshine. In the first year though, we see no visible signs of growth in spite of providing all of these things. In the second year, there is no growth above the soil. The third and fourth years still show no signs of anything happening. In the fifth year something amazing happens. The Chinese bamboo tree grows 90 feet tall in just six weeks.

The children of Israel also had their faith working in five years. Their big harvest was to come only after five years. Perhaps you are doing something and praying for God to bless it. There are certain things that will take five years. That is just the way it is.

Have faith in God! Whether it is three months or five years, God's power will be manifested in your life. Faith is mysterious. It is an unstoppable force. There is no way to tell exactly how fast or how slow things will work out. We serve a living God!

CHAPTER 45

Faith Will Empower You To Subdue Nations

And what shall I more say? For the time would fail me to tell of GIDEON, and of Barak, and of Samson, and of Jephthae; of David also, and Samuel, and of the prophets: WHO THROUGH FAITH SUBDUED KINGDOMS, wrought righteousness, obtained promises, stopped the mouths of lions, Quenched the violence of fire, escaped the edge of the sword, out of weakness were made strong, waxed valiant in fight, turned to flight the armies of the aliens.

Hebrews 11:32-34

Faith Will Empower You To Subdue Nations

Then Jerubbaal, who is Gideon, and all the people that were with him, rose up early, and pitched beside the well of Harod: so that the host of the Midianites were on the north side of them, by the hill of Moreh, in the valley. And the Lord said unto Gideon, The people that are with thee are too many for me to give the Midianites into their hands, lest Israel vaunt themselves against me, saying, Mine own hand hath saved me. Now therefore go to, proclaim in the ears of the people, saying, Whosoever is fearful and afraid, let him return and depart early from mount Gilead. And there returned of the people twenty and two thousand; and there remained ten thousand. And the Lord said unto Gideon, The people are yet too many; bring them down unto the water, and I will try them for thee there: and it shall be, that of whom I say unto thee, This shall go with thee, the same shall go with thee; and of whomsoever I say unto thee, This shall not go with thee, the same shall not go. So he brought down the people unto the water: and the Lord said unto Gideon, Every one that lappeth of the water with his tongue, as a dog lappeth, him shalt thou set by himself; likewise every one that boweth down upon his knees to drink. And the number of them that lapped, putting their hand to their mouth, were three hundred men: but all the rest of the people bowed down upon their knees to drink water. AND THE LORD SAID UNTO GIDEON, BY THE THREE HUNDRED MEN THAT LAPPED WILL I SAVE YOU, AND DELIVER THE MIDIANITES INTO THINE HAND: AND LET ALL THE OTHER PEOPLE GO EVERY MAN UNTO HIS PLACE.

Judges 7:1-7

As you walk in faith, God will use you to take over an entire nation for Him. The heroes of faith subdued entire nations for God. Gideon was one of the heroes of faith and he subdued the Midianites. All he had to do was to believe in God and move forward in faith.

It is very important for you to become a man of faith. You must develop your faith and serve God with joy. The nations of the world are waiting for you. An entire nation has been given to you if only you will be obedient to Him. God will use you to establish churches that will dominate the nations one day.

Many years ago, James McKeon came from Scotland to Ghana. By faith, he subdued the nation through the gospel of Jesus Christ. Today, there are over 2,500 church buildings of his church in Ghana. It is the largest group of church buildings in the nation of Ghana. There are many nations that are far from being subdued by Christ. If you were to walk by faith and believe in your original calling, God would have used you to reach the nations. Instead of believing in the original calling, many Christians have given themselves to secular visions.

They say, "Let us build vocational schools, businesses, banks, universities and hospitals so that we can impact the society." God does not need any help to impact the society. Go across the nations in Africa and you will find that they are not subdued for Christ. Check out Sierra Leone, Senegal, Liberia, Burkina Faso, Chad, Mali, Guinea, Guinea Bissau, Cote d'Ivoire, Togo, Benin, South Africa, Namibia, Cameroon, Congo, and Nigeria. Why are these nations not subdued for Christ? Because no one believed and no one went! Christians are in their various churches celebrating prosperity, achievements and more secular accomplishments. Building human institutions will not subdue nations. Nations are subdued by faith!

It is time to walk by faith and subdue nations for Jesus Christ. God can use you to take an entire nation if you believe and obey Him. Entire nations can be subdued for Christ through you if you believe in Him. Faith is obedience and obedience is faith! Get up and go to the nation God has called you to. Live there! Build the church and build many churches! You will subdue an entire nation for Jesus Christ.

This is why faith is so important. Subduing nations is possible if you believe in the command to go. Instead of doubting whether you have the ability to subdue nations, you must walk on in faith and trust God.

As you step out in faith, you will find yourself subduing nations for God. Have faith in God! Walk by faith! Watch as many preaching videos as you can! Keep listening to messages at home and in the car! It is your master key to subduing nations. He that believeth shall subdue nations for Christ. The more you preach in the nation, the more you subdue it for Christ. The more churches you establish in a nation, the more it is subdued.

CHAPTER 46

Faith Enables You to Overcome Superior Enemies

And what shall I more say? for the time would fail me to tell of Gedeon, AND OF BARAK, and of Samson, and of Jephthae; of David also, and Samuel, and of the prophets: Who through faith subdued kingdoms, wrought righteousness, obtained promises, stopped the mouths of lions, Quenched the violence of fire, escaped the edge of the sword, out of weakness were made strong, waxed valiant in fight, turned to flight the armies of the aliens.

Hebrews 11:32-34

Faith Enables You to Overcome Superior Enemies

1. **By faith you will overcome superior enemies. Barak overcame 900 chariots of iron of Sisera.**

   And the Lord sold them into the hand of Jabin king of Canaan, that reigned in Hazor; the captain of whose host was Sisera, which dwelt in Harosheth of the Gentiles. And the children of Israel cried unto the Lord: FOR HE HAD NINE HUNDRED CHARIOTS OF IRON; AND TWENTY YEARS HE MIGHTILY OPPRESSED THE CHILDREN OF ISRAEL.

   Judges 4:2-3

2. **By faith you will overcome superior enemies. Barak overcame twenty years of oppression and struggling.**

   And the Lord sold them into the hand of Jabin king of Canaan, that reigned in Hazor; the captain of whose host was Sisera, which dwelt in Harosheth of the Gentiles. And the children of Israel cried unto the Lord: for he had nine hundred chariots of iron; and TWENTY YEARS HE MIGHTILY OPPRESSED THE CHILDREN OF ISRAEL.

   Judges 4:2-3

3. **By faith you will overcome superior enemies. Barak chased his enemy away.** By faith you will chase away the ones who have been tormenting you. Your faith will make your worst enemy runaway from you.

   And the Lord discomfited Sisera, and all his chariots, and all his host, with the edge of the sword before Barak; so that Sisera lighted down off his chariot, and fled away on his feet. BUT BARAK PURSUED AFTER THE CHARIOTS, and after the host, unto Harosheth of the Gentiles: and all the host of Sisera fell upon the edge of the sword; and there was not a man left.

   Judges 4:15-16

Barak is listed as one of the heroes of faith. Most people do not know what he did to join this prestigious list. In the scriptures, you will see that Barak overcame a superior enemy who had oppressed them for many years.

Many wars are fought between one superior party and one vastly inferior enemy. That is often the reason why the war starts. Someone thinks he can overcome you, bully you and easily defeat you. Then he declares war on you.

Today, you may be facing a vastly superior enemy; something that oppresses you and makes your life miserable.

Whatever makes you cry will be defeated by faith! Every situation that the enemy is using to mock you will turn around by faith. All your mockers will perish and you will hear of them running away in the name of Jesus!

Your enemy will be found naked and fleeing, to the astonishment of all who watched you being oppressed and harassed. How could such a turnaround take place?

Why will the Goliath in your life fall to the ground? Once again, there is no natural explanation. Faith is an unstoppable force! Faith unleashes an invisible power that can change the course of nature. Jesus would have drowned in the Sea of Galilee, just as people still drown in that lake today. Through his faith, he unleashed an unstoppable force. He partnered with an invisible power to accomplish a great victory. This is how Barak overcame his superior enemy. Barak chased away an army which had superior technology. Barak chased away an army which had a massive high-tech war machine.

Barak chased away an enemy who had not been defeated for twenty years. Barak overcame a superior, wicked, oppressive and malevolent enemy. This will be your story! Whatever power is over your head, pushing you under the water is rebuked today. The evil eye that looks upon you to finish you off goes blind in the name of Jesus! You are declared victorious! Not by might nor by power! An invisible force will fight for you and cut off the arms of your oppressor. The legs of your superior enemy will be chopped off in the name of Jesus! A slicing power will cut your enemy into pieces. You will not have to fight in this battle in the name of Jesus!

Please notice the amazing scriptures that describe the victories of Barak. That is how your victories will also be described! That is how people will talk about you! That is how people will recount your victories! You will be used as a good example of someone who overcame superior enemies! Walk by faith and experience victory over every type of senior, superior, greater, higher, bigger, grander and more experienced enemy.

CHAPTER 47

Faith Overcomes Rejection

And what shall I more say? for the time would fail me to tell of Gedeon, and of Barak, and of Samson, and of JEPHTHAE; of David also, and Samuel, and of the prophets: Who through faith subdued kingdoms, wrought righteousness, obtained promises, stopped the mouths of lions, Quenched the violence of fire, escaped the edge of the sword, out of weakness were made strong, waxed valiant in fight, turned to flight the armies of the aliens.

Hebrews 11:32-34

1. **Faith overcomes rejection: By faith you will overcome your difficult background.** By faith you will overcome all the rejection that comes in your life. Jephthah was the son of a harlot. He was rejected by the family.

   Now Jephthah the Gileadite was a mighty man of valour, and he was the son of an harlot: and Gilead begat Jephthah. And Gilead's wife bare him sons; and his wife's sons grew up, and they thrust out Jephthah, and said unto him, THOU SHALT NOT INHERIT IN OUR FATHER'S HOUSE; FOR THOU ART THE SON OF A STRANGE WOMAN. Then Jephthah fled from his brethren, and dwelt in the land of Tob: and there were gathered vain men to Jephthah, and went out with him.

   Judges 11:1-3

2. **Faith overcomes rejection: By faith you will forgive those who offended you and become a saviour to men.**

   And it came to pass in process of time, that the children of Ammon made war against Israel. And it was so, that when the children of Ammon made war against Israel, the elders of Gilead went to fetch Jephthah out of the land of Tob: And they said unto Jephthah, Come, and be our captain, that we may fight with the children of Ammon. AND JEPHTHAH SAID UNTO THE ELDERS OF GILEAD, DID NOT YE HATE ME, AND EXPEL ME OUT OF MY FATHER'S HOUSE? AND WHY ARE YE COME UNTO ME NOW WHEN YE ARE IN DISTRESS? And the elders of Gilead said unto Jephthah, Therefore we turn again to thee now, that thou mayest go with us, and fight against the children of Ammon, and be our head over all the inhabitants of Gilead. And Jephthah said unto the elders of Gilead, If ye bring me home again to fight against the children of Ammon, and the Lord deliver them before me, shall I be your head? And the elders of Gilead said unto Jephthah, The Lord be witness between us, if we do not so according to thy words.

   Judges 11:4-10

3. **Faith overcomes rejection: By faith you will make promises and keep them.** You will make promises to God and to man and will keep them. Jephthah vowed to give anything that came out to meet him when he came back from a victorious campaign.

Then the Spirit of the Lord came upon Jephthah, and he passed over Gilead, and Manasseh, and passed over Mizpeh of Gilead, and from Mizpeh of Gilead he passed over unto the children of Ammon. And Jephthah vowed a vow unto the Lord, and said, If thou shalt without fail deliver the children of Ammon into mine hands, Then it shall be, that whatsoever cometh forth of the doors of my house to meet me, when I return in peace from the children of Ammon, shall surely be the Lord's, and I will offer it up for a burnt offering.

Judges 11:29-31

CHAPTER 48

Faith Will Turn Your Weaknesses into Strength

Who through faith subdued kingdoms, wrought righteousness, obtained promises, stopped the mouths of lions, Quenched the violence of fire, escaped the edge of the sword, OUT OF WEAKNESS WERE MADE STRONG, waxed valiant in fight, turned to flight the armies of the aliens.

Hebrews 11:33-34

By faith your weakness will be turned into strength. The weakness of your life will be made strong. By faith the enemy who threatens you will start running away from you very fast. Whatever threatens you will be made to flee from you. The weakness of Jehoshaphat is clearly seen in the prayer that he prayed, "We have no might." Even though Jehoshaphat was weak, he stood up with the little ones, the children and the wives and called on God.

Out of his weakness, he was made strong. Out of weakness, he turned away the armies of the enemy. God gave them more than they could carry! No matter how weak you are today, you will be made strong! Strength will come into your life through your faith in God. The armies of the devil will turn around and flee from you. It is important that you read the story from the Bible and you will see how faith turned to flight the armies of the aliens.

> Behold, I say, how they reward us, to come to cast us out of thy possession, which thou hast given us to inherit. O our God, wilt thou not judge them? FOR WE HAVE NO MIGHT AGAINST THIS GREAT COMPANY THAT COMETH AGAINST US; NEITHER KNOW WE WHAT TO DO: BUT OUR EYES ARE UPON THEE. AND ALL JUDAH STOOD BEFORE THE LORD, WITH THEIR LITTLE ONES, THEIR WIVES, AND THEIR CHILDREN. Then upon Jahaziel the son of Zechariah, the son of Benaiah, the son of Jeiel, the son of Mattaniah, a Levite of the sons of Asaph, came the Spirit of the Lord in the midst of the congregation; And he said, Hearken ye, all Judah, and ye inhabitants of Jerusalem, and thou king Jehoshaphat, Thus saith the Lord unto you, Be not afraid nor dismayed by reason of this great multitude; for the battle is not yours, but God's. To morrow go ye down against them: behold, they come up by the cliff of Ziz; and ye shall find them at the end of the brook, before the wilderness of Jeruel. Ye shall not need to fight in this battle: set yourselves, stand ye still, and see the salvation of the Lord with you, O Judah and Jerusalem: fear not, nor

be dismayed; to morrow go out against them: for the Lord will be with you.

And Jehoshaphat bowed his head with his face to the ground: and all Judah and the inhabitants of Jerusalem fell before the Lord, worshipping the Lord. And the Levites, of the children of the Kohathites, and of the children of the Korhites, stood up to praise the Lord God of Israel with a loud voice on high.

And they rose early in the morning, and went forth into the wilderness of Tekoa: and as they went forth, Jehoshaphat stood and said, Hear me, O Judah, and ye inhabitants of Jerusalem; Believe in the Lord your God, so shall ye be established; believe his prophets, so shall ye prosper. And when he had consulted with the people, he appointed singers unto the Lord, and that should praise the beauty of holiness, as they went out before the army, and to say, Praise the Lord; for his mercy endureth for ever. And when they began to sing and to praise, THE LORD SET AMBUSHMENTS AGAINST THE CHILDREN OF AMMON, MOAB, AND MOUNT SEIR, WHICH WERE COME AGAINST JUDAH; AND THEY WERE SMITTEN. For the children of Ammon and Moab stood up against the inhabitants of mount Seir, utterly to slay and destroy them: and when they had made an end of the inhabitants of Seir, every one helped to destroy another.

And when Judah came toward the watch tower in the wilderness, they looked unto the multitude, and, behold, they were dead bodies fallen to the earth, and none escaped. AND WHEN JEHOSHAPHAT AND HIS PEOPLE CAME TO TAKE AWAY THE SPOIL OF THEM, THEY FOUND AMONG THEM IN ABUNDANCE BOTH RICHES WITH THE DEAD BODIES, AND PRECIOUS JEWELS, WHICH THEY STRIPPED OFF FOR THEMSELVES, MORE THAN THEY COULD CARRY AWAY: and they were three days in gathering of the spoil, it was so much.

2 Chronicles 20:11-25

Keep listening to messages! Keep listening to preaching! Your faith is growing without you realising it. The armies of the aliens will run from you. You are far stronger because of your faith. You are far greater because of your faith. Faith makes you bigger than all the armies that have surrounded you. Faith makes you escape from the trap you find yourself in. Faith is your master key to overcoming the superior enemies that surround you. Faith brings in angels and invisible forces to fight on your side. Faith is a weapon! Faith is an unstoppable force! Faith is partnering with the invisible to accomplish the impossible!

CHAPTER 49

Faith Is Operating with the Consciousness of the Invisible

BY FAITH he forsook Egypt, not fearing the wrath of the king: for he endured, as SEEING HIM WHO IS INVISIBLE.

Hebrews 11:27

Faith is operating with the consciousness of the invisible. A consciousness of the presence of God invokes the invisible God to intervene. The more faith you have, the more you will be conscious of the invisible world.

Moses was a great giant of faith because he saw the invisible. He was conscious of what could not be seen with the natural eye.

A man of faith is conscious of God's presence. As you walk about, you will sense the rich presence of God. People who have no faith are oblivious to the reality of God's presence.

A man of faith is conscious of the presence of Jesus Christ. There are times I sense the presence of God and I know that Jesus is present. Even without seeing Jesus you can sense His presence. There was a time I was walking up and down in my study and I felt the presence of Jesus. He gave me a word that was so contrary to my knowledge that I was forced to check it up in the Bible. The presence of Jesus is real but only a man of faith can enjoy that presence.

A man of faith is conscious of the presence of angels. Angels are as real as human beings. From time to time, you will become conscious of the presence of angels. Without faith you will never be conscious of the presence of angels. One day whilst in Scotland, I suddenly felt the presence of an angel in my room. I received a message from the Lord, which guided me along a special road. I did not see anything but I was so sure of the presence of this angel. It was to strengthen me in my battles against demonic hordes.

A man of faith is conscious of the presence of evil spirits. Demons are as real as human beings. There are thousands of evil spirits roaming the earth today looking for somewhere to dwell. I once sensed the presence of an evil spirit in a hotel room. When you have faith, you will sense different types of evil in different places. One day, I felt the presence of blood that had been shed all over the floor of a house I was staying in. That was a spirit of murder and bloodshed. Evil spirits are real and it is time to deal with them as you walk by faith.

Enjoying the presence of God and the ministry of angels is possible if you are a faith person. Receive grace to enjoy the presence of God. Receive grace to enjoy the presence of angels.

Conquering devils is possible if you believe in the Word. Instead of doubting whether these things are real, you must walk on in faith and trust God. As you step out in faith, you will find yourself quenching the wickedness of evil powers around you. Demons are hoping that you will never notice them! Demons are hoping that you will never say anything about them! Demons are hoping that you will never bind them. Every time you bind an evil spirit, it is tied with spiritual steel twine. Every time you bind devils, they are gagged, neutralized and paralysed. By faith, become conscious of the presence of the invisible and deal with the enemy.

Have faith in God! Walk by faith! Watch as many preaching videos as you can! It will help to open your eyes. Keep listening to messages all the time. Keep listening to important preaching as though your life depends on it. Faith comes by hearing!

Faith is your master key to God's presence. Faith is your master key to neutralizing the presence of evil powers that have surrounded your house.

CHAPTER 50

Faith Is Partnering with the Invisible to Accomplish the Impossible

And these three men, Shadrach, Meshach, and Abednego, fell down bound into the midst of the burning fiery furnace. Then Nebuchadnezzar the king was astonied, and rose up in haste, and spake, and said unto his counsellors, Did not we cast three men bound into the midst of the fire? They answered and said unto the king, True, O king. He answered and said, Lo, I SEE FOUR MEN LOOSE, WALKING IN THE MIDST OF THE FIRE, and they have no hurt; and the form of the fourth is like the Son of God.

Daniel 3:23-25

When Shadrach, Meshach and Abednego were thrown into the fire, some invisible force must have prevented them from being burnt. Indeed, there was an invisible power working with the three men. King Nebuchadnezzar saw the fourth man who was invisible to others.

There is an invisible power partnering with every man of faith.

By faith he forsook Egypt, not fearing the wrath of the king: for he endured, as seeing him who IS INVISIBLE. Through faith he kept the passover, and the sprinkling of blood, lest he that destroyed the firstborn should touch them.

By faith they PASSED THROUGH THE RED SEA as by dry land: which the Egyptians assaying to do were drowned.

By faith the WALLS OF JERICHO FELL DOWN, after they were compassed about seven days.

Hebrews 11:27-30

Faith is the creating of an active partnership with the invisible to accomplish the incredible.

The stories of the heroes of faith inspire us greatly. You can sense that there is a partnership between a human being and an invisible force. When Moses passed through the Red Sea, there must have been some invisible force that pushed back the waters. When the walls of Jericho fell down, there must have been some invisible force that pushed them down.

When Daniel was in the lions' den, some invisible force must have shut the mouths of the lions.

And what shall I more say? for the time would fail me to tell of Gedeon, and of Barak, and of Samson, and of Jephthae; of David also, and Samuel, and of the prophets: Who through faith subdued kingdoms, wrought righteousness, obtained promises, stopped the mouths of lions, Quenched the violence of fire, escaped the edge of the sword, out of weakness were made strong, waxed valiant in fight, turned to flight the armies of the aliens.

Hebrews 11:32-34

All the people in the list above; Gideon, Barak, Samson, Jepthae, David and Samuel cooperated with an invisible power to accomplish the incredible and the impossible.

Do you see why faith is so important? Through faith you can have an invisible partner to help you accomplish the impossible. Incredible and impossible works only happen if you walk by faith.

Instead of doubting whether these stories are true or not, you must walk on in faith and trust God. As you step out in faith, you will find yourself partnering with the invisible to accomplish the impossible.

Have faith in God! Walk by faith! Watch as many preaching videos as you can! Keep listening to messages at home. It is your master key to doing greater works. He that believeth shall do amazing works for the Lord. Soon, your name will be in a new list of heroes of faith.

Most of the things I have accomplished in the ministry are humanly impossible. A minister based in Ghana is not likely to accomplish certain things. A worldwide ministry is usually an impossible achievement for someone who comes from a highly indebted and poor country. Faith is partnering with the invisible to accomplish the impossible!

Allow yourself to be inspired as you listen to preaching every day. Faith comes by hearing and hearing comes by the word of God. You will accomplish the impossible in the name of Jesus! There is an invisible force partnering with every man of faith.

CHAPTER 51

Faith is a Power that Converts Defeat to Victory

For whatsoever is born of God overcometh the world: and this is the victory that overcometh the world, even our faith.

1 John 5:4

Faith Secrets

Faith is a converter! Faith converts your defeats into victories.

Faith is the converter of the natural into the supernatural. Like Daniel you are converted into an "uneatable" person. Faith converts defeat to victory.

Daniel was defeated in court. He was found guilty of subverting the king's command. He was thrown into prison and sentenced to a horrible death. Everyone was expecting that he would be torn into pieces by hungry lions that had not eaten for days. Faith converted his defeat in court into a victory. This is the victory that overcomes the world. Faith is indeed a converter!

Life is a long journey. There are many instances where you will feel that you have been defeated. You may feel that you have lost the war and lost the battle. Your faith will turn things around. Faith will convert the defeat into victory. Continue to speak positive things about your destiny in God. As you declare the Word, it will come to pass. You will be rescued from the lion's den. Your defeat will be converted into a stunning victory.

Do you feel you have been defeated in marriage? Perhaps, all your efforts have gone down the drain. Walk by faith and not by sight. You are going to come out victorious. Has someone taken you to court? Are you engaged in a battle with someone for something? Maintain your faith. Faith is very important for the battle. You cannot experience victory except you have faith. This is the victory that overcomes, even your faith. Faith is a source of victory. Faith will give you the upper hand!

Do you see why faith is so important? Faith is a source of victory. Through faith your defeat will be converted into a victory. An unstoppable force will give you a seemingly impossible victory.

Instead of questioning and doubting God's word, you must walk on in faith and trust the Word. As you step out in faith, your apparent defeat will be converted into a series of victories. Have faith in God! Walk by faith! Faith comes by hearing and hearing comes by the word of God. Keep coming to church. Listen to the messages over and over. Listen to old messages and new messages. Faith will work for you!

Watch as many preaching videos as you can! Watching all these videos makes you a man of faith. Keep listening to messages at home, at school and at work. Listen to the word of God whilst you are walking and whilst you are working. Faith is your master key to converting your defeat into victory. This is the victory that overcomes the world – your faith!

CHAPTER 52

Faith is a Power that Converts Sickness to Health

The same heard Paul speak: who stedfastly beholding him, and perceiving that he had faith to be healed,

Acts 14:9

Faith converts sickness into health!

Faith is a converter! Faith converts your sickness into health.

All through the gospels, Jesus healed people that had faith in Him. Jesus always told the people that their faith had made them whole.

> And he said unto her, DAUGHTER, THY FAITH HATH MADE THEE WHOLE; go in peace, and be whole of thy plague.
>
> Mark 5:34

> And they came to Jericho: and as he went out of Jericho with his disciples and a great number of people, blind Bartimaeus, the son of Timaeus, sat by the highway side begging. And when he heard that it was Jesus of Nazareth, he began to cry out, and say, Jesus, thou Son of David, have mercy on me. And many charged him that he should hold his peace: but he cried the more a great deal, Thou Son of David, have mercy on me. And Jesus stood still, and commanded him to be called. And they call the blind man, saying unto him, be of good comfort, rise; he calleth thee. And he, casting away his garment, rose, and came to Jesus. And Jesus answered and said unto him, what wilt thou that I should do unto thee? - The blind man said unto him, Lord, that I might receive my sight. And Jesus said unto him, Go thy way; THY FAITH HATH MADE THEE WHOLE. And immediately he received his sight, and followed Jesus in the way.
>
> Mark 10:46-52

> And Jesus answering said, were there not ten cleansed? But where are the nine? There are not found that returned to give glory to God, save this stranger. And he said unto him, Arise, go thy way: THY FAITH HATH MADE THEE WHOLE.
>
> Luke 17:17-19

Faith Secrets

Faith is the converter of the natural into the supernatural. Like the woman with the issue of blood, your sickness will be converted into health. Faith converts sickness into health!

I do not know what sickness you are encountering. I can assure you that medical science is also limited in what it can do. At any miracle service, most of the people desiring a healing have already been attended to by medical doctors. The conditions they bring to miracle services are what they have after medical science has done its very best.

No matter how you criticise faith healers, there will always be people seeking healing. The woman with the issue of blood had already seen many physicians. Today, people have suffered many things from many physicians. But they still need healing.

Faith in God will never be out-dated or useless! Faith in God will always be a necessary weapon.

Life is a long journey. There are many instances where you will fall sick. You will always need your faith to turn things around. Continue to speak positive things about God's destiny. As you declare the Word, it will come to pass. You will be rescued from every evil sickness. You will be delivered from evil diagnoses. Your unwell-feeling will be converted into brilliant health.

Maintain your faith. Faith is very important for the battle of life. Remember these words: "Thy faith hath made thee whole"! You will experience long life through your faith. People who have faith usually live longer than those who have no faith. Faith has an effect on your health. Faith pleases God. This is the victory that overcomes, even your faith. Faith is a source of healing. Faith will give you the upper hand! Faith converts sickness into health. Faith makes you whole!

CHAPTER 53

Faith is a Power that Converts Barrenness into Fruitfulness

THROUGH FAITH ALSO SARA HERSELF RECEIVED STRENGTH to conceive seed, and was delivered of a child when she was past age, because she judged him faithful who had promised. Therefore sprang there even of one, and him as good as dead, so many as the stars of the sky in multitude, and as the sand which is by the sea shore innumerable.

Hebrews 11:11-12

Faith converts barrenness to fruitfulness.

Faith is the game changer! Faith is the converter of the natural into the supernatural. Like Sarah, you will receive strength to conceive. Your barrenness will be converted into fruitfulness. Faith converts sickness into health!

I do not know what kind of barrenness you are encountering. I can assure you that medical science is also limited in what it can do. Medical doctors have attended to most barren women desiring healing. Yet, many have no solution.

The continued barrenness of many is what they experience after medical science has done its best. No matter how you criticise faith healers, there will always be women seeking help. Many women have already been attended to by doctors. Whether they have seen doctors or not, they still need the Lord's help.

Faith in God will never be out-dated or useless! Faith in God will always be a necessary weapon.

Life is a long journey. There are many people who will need prayer. Many women cannot have children. We will always need faith to turn things around. Continue to speak positive things about God's destiny. As you declare the Word, it will come to pass. You will be rescued from every evil diagnoses. You will be delivered from evil spirits. Your barrenness will be converted into twins and triplets. Watch this wonderful prophecy;

> Sing, O barren, thou that didst not bear; break forth into singing, and cry aloud, thou that didst not travail with child: for more are the children of the desolate than the children of the married wife, saith the Lord.
>
> Enlarge the place of thy tent, and let them stretch forth the curtains of thine habitations: spare not, lengthen thy cords, and strengthen thy stakes;
>
> For thou shalt break forth on the right hand and on the left; and thy seed shall inherit the Gentiles, and make the desolate cities to be inhabited.

Fear not; for thou shalt not be ashamed: neither be thou confounded; for thou shalt not be put to shame: for thou shalt forget the shame of thy youth, and shalt not remember the reproach of thy widowhood any more.

Isaiah 54:1-4

Maintain your faith. Faith is very important for the battle. You will experience a long life through your faith. People who have faith usually live longer than those who have no faith. Faith has an effect on your health. Faith pleases God. This is the victory that overcomes, even your faith. Faith is a source of healing. Faith will give you the upper hand!

Fruitfulness is possible if you believe the word of God. Instead of doubting the scripture, you must walk on in faith and trust God. As you step out in faith, you will find yourself doing greater works than your fathers. Have faith in God! Walk by faith! Watch as many preaching videos as you can! Keep listening to messages in the house, at work and in school! It is your master key to fruitfulness. He that believeth shall become fruitful. The more preaching you listen to, the more likely you are to become fruitful.

When you hear preaching on miracles and healing, your faith in miracles and healing will rise. Faith comes by hearing and hearing comes by the word of God. As you listen to sermons on the power of God, you will find yourself believing in God. Your barrenness will be converted into fruitfulness in the name of Jesus!

CHAPTER 54

Faith is a Power that Converts Failure into Success

And Simon answering said unto him, Master, we have toiled all the night, and have taken nothing: nevertheless at thy word I will let down the net. And when they had this done, they inclosed a great multitude of fishes: and their net brake. And they beckoned unto their partners, which were in the other ship, that they should come and help them. And they came, and filled both the ships, so that they began to sink. When Simon Peter saw it, he fell down at Jesus' knees, saying, depart from me; for I am a sinful man, O Lord.

Luke 5:5-8

Faith converts failure to success!

Faith is a converter! Faith converts your failures into successes.

Faith is the converter of the natural into the supernatural.

Simon was not successful at fishing that night. He worked and toiled all night and got very little out of it. Simon was an expert at fishing. He owned his own boat. He employed several people. He was experienced but he was still a failure. When he had a word from Jesus, he decided to believe the word. His abysmal failure was converted into a brilliant success.

Daniel tried to argue his way in court but he was outdone. Faith always converts failure to success. Daniel failed in court. He was found guilty of subverting the king's command. He was thrown into prison and sentenced to a horrible death. Everyone was expecting that he would be torn into pieces by hungry lions that had not eaten for days. Faith converted his failure into a success story. You will have a success story too!

There are many instances where you will feel that you are a failure. You may feel that you have lost the war and lost the battle. But your faith will turn things around. Continue to speak positive things about God's destiny. As you declare the Word, it will come to pass. You will be rescued from the lion's den. Your defeat will be converted into a stunning victory.

Walk by faith and not by sight. You are going to come out victorious. Have you taken an examination and failed? Did you fail your driving test? Maintain your faith. Faith is very important for the battle. You cannot experience success without God's help. This is the victory that overcomes, even your faith. Faith is a source of success. Faith will give you the upper hand!

Do you see why faith is so important? Through faith your failure will be converted into a success. An unstoppable force will give you a seemingly impossible victory.

Instead of questioning and doubting God's word, you must walk on in faith and trust the Word. As you step out in faith, your failures will be converted into successes. Have faith in God! Walk by faith! Faith comes by hearing and hearing comes by the word of God. Keep coming to church. Listen to the messages over and over. Listen to old messages and new messages. Your faith is converting your failure into stunning victories.

Watch as many preaching videos as you can! Keep listening to messages at home, at school and at work. Listen to the word of God whilst you are walking and whilst you are working. It is your master key to converting your many failures into a marvellous success story.

CHAPTER 55

Faith Converts a Wicked Man into a Good Man

Even when we were dead in sins, hath quickened us together with Christ, (by grace ye are saved;) And hath raised us up together, and made us sit together in heavenly places in Christ Jesus: That in the ages to come he might shew the exceeding riches of his grace in his kindness toward us through Christ Jesus. For by grace are ye SAVED THROUGH FAITH; and that not of yourselves: it is the gift of God:

Ephesians 2:5-8

Faith Secrets

Faith converts a dead wicked, evil sinner into a living saint. Truly, we were dead in sins and separated from God. We had no hope in this life or in the after life. It seems as though the human race has gone through a mutation and has become a helplessly wicked and malevolent race.

Faith is a converter! Faith converts sinners into righteous men.

Faith is the converter of the corrupt into the incorruptible.

Paul was not a good person. He persecuted the church of God. He supervised the murder of an anointed pastor. He was full of an evil zeal and blasphemy. Yet, when he found faith in Christ, he was converted into one of the greatest apostles. Faith converts wicked people into righteous men. The salvation of Paul through faith is a pattern which is repeated throughout the ages. Many wicked men have turned to God by the simple act of faith.

> And I thank Christ Jesus our Lord, who hath enabled me, for that he counted me faithful, putting me into the ministry; Who was before a blasphemer, and a persecutor, and injurious: but I obtained mercy, because I did it ignorantly in unbelief. And the grace of our Lord was exceeding abundant with faith and love which is in Christ Jesus. This is a faithful saying, and worthy of all acceptation, that Christ Jesus came into the world to save sinners; of whom I am chief. Howbeit for this cause I obtained mercy, that in me first Jesus Christ might shew forth all longsuffering, for A PATTERN TO THEM WHICH SHOULD HEREAFTER BELIEVE on him to life everlasting.
>
> 1 Timothy 1:12-16

The thief on the cross was a thief! He was not an allegorical thief. He was a real thief. Yet, when he turned his heart towards Jesus and believed in Him, he received instant miracle salvation. "You will be with me in paradise," were the famous words Jesus spoke to him. Faith converts wicked men into righteous men.

There are many instances where you will feel that you are a sinner. You may feel that you have lost your fight against sin.

You are justified and made righteous by faith and not by your works. Faith is what has converted you from a wicked sinner to a righteous man.

Therefore being justified by faith, we have peace with God through our Lord Jesus Christ:
Romans 5:1

Continue to speak positive things about your salvation. As you declare the Word, it will come to pass. You will be rescued from falling into the devil's condemnation.

Do you feel you are failing in your quest to live righteously? I'm sure you do because that is how I also feel. In spite of all your efforts, you keep falling back into the same mess. Walk by faith and not by sight. You are going to come out victorious. You are not righteous because of the things you have done and not done. You are righteous because of your faith. Faith is what has converted you into a righteous man.

Knowing that A MAN IS NOT JUSTIFIED BY THE WORKS OF THE LAW, but by the faith of Jesus Christ, even we have believed in Jesus Christ, that we might be justified by the faith of Christ, and not by the works of the law: for by the works of the law shall no flesh be justified.
Galatians 2:16

Faith is an unstoppable force that will keep you walking with God. Instead of questioning and doubting God's word, you must walk on in faith and trust the Word. As you step out in faith, your sinful lifestyle will be converted into righteousness. Have faith in God! Walk by faith! Faith comes by hearing and hearing comes by the word of God. Keep coming to church. Listen to the messages over and over. Listen to old messages and new messages. You are changing into a righteous man!

Watch as many preaching videos as you can! Keep listening to messages at home, at school and at work. Listen to the word of God whilst you are walking and whilst you are working. It is your master key to walking and living in the righteousness of God.

CHAPTER 56

Faith Converts You into a Hard Worker

There remaineth therefore a rest to the people of God. For he that is entered into his rest, he also hath ceased from his own works, as God did from his. LET US LABOUR therefore to enter into that rest, LEST ANY MAN FALL AFTER THE SAME EXAMPLE OF UNBELIEF.

Hebrews 4:9-11

Faith Converts You into a Hard Worker

Let us labour! Let us labour! Let us work hard! Let us work hard!

That is faith! To work hard is to show your faith.

A hard-working tireless person has something on his mind. Perhaps, he has a reward on his mind. Perhaps he expects some fruits. His desire for fruitfulness will spur him on. His desire to please his boss will urge him on. His faith in his boss' response will make him work harder still.

Let us labour! Let us labour! Let us work hard! Let us work hard!

That is faith! To work hard is to show your faith.

Those who want to do the work of God at weekends do not really believe that eternity holds immense rewards for us.

Those who reject the call of God to labour in his vineyard do not really believe that this world is not our home. They would rather work very hard for a godless unbeliever than to work for God. When it comes to the work of God, all they can do is to attend one church service a week.

Those who have faith heed the call. They hear the invitation and they say, "Here I am, send me. Use me! Put me to work!"

Let us labour! Let us labour! Let us work hard! Let us work hard!

That is faith! To work hard is to show your faith.

Those who have faith know that our labour is not in vain in the Lord. They believe that they should be steadfast, unmoveable, always abounding in the work of the Lord. Why? Because they have faith in the word of God.

Today, the church is full of lazy bones who are not prepared to do anything for God. "Give me a new car! Give me a new job! Fill my empty hands! I lift them up to You, O Lord. Fill my wardrobe with clothes so that I can show them off at the next party."

That is Christianity today! The harvest is plenty but those who labour are few. Those who labour are those who have faith. The fields are white unto harvest. The labourers are few. The men of faith are few. Are you one of them?

Let us labour so that we do not fall into unbelief! Let us work hard so that we do not fall into faithlessness!

To have faith is to work hard. To have faith is to live for God. Faith is to labour and to work very hard for the Lord. To not work hard is the sign of your lack of faith.

The more you believe in the word of God, the harder you will work. Your hard work is the evidence of your faith!

CHAPTER 57

Faith is Precious

Simon Peter, a servant and an apostle of Jesus Christ, to them that have obtained like PRECIOUS FAITH with us through the righteousness of God and our Saviour Jesus Christ:

2 Peter 1:1

Faith Secrets

Faith is a precious thing because it brings you back into favour with God. Human beings are a group of created beings that have lost favour with God. It is as though there has been a major genetic mutation that has brought a spontaneous evil nature into all men. Without effort, men are filled with evil, deficiencies, moral failings, shortcomings and ill will. Evil spews out of all men without any provocation.

Human beings are best described as a disappointment to their Creator. Indeed, God repented that He had made man and decided to drown every single one of His created beings.

With the release of earthquakes, the fountains of the deep were unlocked and huge tidal waves came over the earth. Millions and millions of people perished but Noah was favoured to escape this judgment. The rest of the human race are products of this righteous Noah.

Unfortunately, after Noah, the perversion of the human race into a complicated and malevolent army of corrupt beings has continued. Jesus Himself predicted that the end of the world would be just like the days of Noah. Human beings have gone full cycle and have descended again into a darkened condition, meriting total annihilation. It is evident that the human race will be wiped out again.

Who, within the human race, can find favour with an angry and disappointed Creator? Indeed, if there is any way we could appease our Creator's disappointment and disillusionment, we should find it. Jesus Christ came as a last ditch effort to prevent the wiping out of the human race again. He offered to the human race a simple key that would lead to the rescuing of the human race. Faith! The rescue of human beings by faith is what we call salvation.

Through faith a great rescue will take place and many will find favour with God before the gavel falls.

Faith, believing in God, and not any acts of righteousness, is the only basis for finding favour with God. Faith is a very important thing as far as God is concerned. Through faith, you are saved, made righteous and justified before God. Indeed, God seems to actually like you when you have faith.

Instead of God trying to drown you or burn you, you become His favoured child. All this is possible through faith. This amazing favour with God has come about through faith. Let us see how faith brings you into favour with God.

1. Faith Gives You Salvation.

> For by grace are ye saved through faith; and that not of yourselves: it is the gift of God:
>
> Ephesians 2:8

> For God sent not his Son into the world to condemn the world; but that the world through him might be saved. He that believeth on him is not condemned: but he that believeth not is condemned already, because he hath not believed in the name of the only begotten Son of God.
>
> John 3:17-18

2. Faith Makes You Righteous and Justified.

> Therefore we conclude that a man is justified by faith without the deeds of the law.
>
> Romans 3:28

> But before faith came, we were kept under the law, shut up unto the faith which should afterwards be revealed. Wherefore the law was our schoolmaster to bring us unto Christ, that we might be justified by faith.
>
> Galatians 3:23-24

3. Faith Makes You A Child Of God.

> He came unto his own, and his own received him not. But as many as received him, to them gave he power to become the sons of God, even to them that believe on his name:
>
> John 1:11-12

4. Faith Makes You Please God.

But without faith it is impossible to please him: for he that cometh to God must believe that he is, and that he is a rewarder of them that diligently seek him.

Hebrews 11:6

5. Faith Makes You Walk With God.

(For we walk by faith, not by sight)

2 Corinthians 5:7

6. Faith Makes You Have Rewards In Heaven.

I have fought a good fight, I have finished my course, I have kept the faith: Henceforth there is laid up for me a crown of righteousness, which the Lord, the righteous judge, shall give me at that day: and not to me only, but unto all them also that love his appearing.

2 Timothy 4:7-8

Faith is a wonderful key that will change everything about your life. Keep stirring up your faith. Faith will really help you and give you favour with God. Faith is your secret weapon! Faith comes by hearing and hearing comes by the word of God. The more you listen to preaching, the more you hear the Word, the more your faith is built up! Keep developing your faith by listening even more to preaching and teaching.

You will have great favour with God as you develop your faith. Faith is the only thing that will work for you. We are saved by faith! Faith is precious to us!

CHAPTER 58

Faith Grafts You In

Thou wilt say then, the branches were broken off, that I MIGHT BE GRAFFED IN. Well; because of unbelief they were broken off, and thou standest BY FAITH. Be not highminded, but fear:

Romans 11:19-20

Faith Secrets

Faith is a grafting power that attaches an unwanted branch to another tree. Faith is a grafting power that causes you to belong to something that you do not qualify for. Faith is a grafting power that attaches you permanently to a new and living source of life. Faith is a grafting power that adds a dying, withered branch to a successful living tree.

Faith is a grafting power that pulls in those who do not belong anywhere. *Faith is a grafting power that adds an outsider to an existing group.*

Faith is therefore a grafting power that will join you to a group that you don't belong to. Faith will graft you into a higher and greater family.

Your salvation is the first manifestation of this grafting power. You originally belong to a group of perishing outsiders. You originally belong to a group of wicked sinners that should be in hell. You originally belong to the liars, the thieves and the fornicators of this world who are destined for damnation. You really belong to a group of demonized witches, wizards and demon-possessed people who are going straight into hell fire.

You belong to the godless men and women of this world who do not fear God. You truly belong to the group of drunkards, drug addicts and hopelessly lost individuals who do not know anything about God. You belong to the religious hypocrites who pretend to be good on the outside but are evil within. Indeed, this is the group of people that you truly belong to. And yet, through salvation, you are grafted into a completely different group.

By the grafting power of faith you have been attached to a group of saints. By the grafting power of faith, you have been attached to people heading for heaven. By the grafting power of faith, you are joined to the church of Jesus Christ. By the grafting power of faith, you are pulled into the elect, the saved, the washed, the rescued and the redeemed of the Lord.

You have not been grafted into this group because of your financial standing. Your money has nothing to do with this. Your family connections have nothing to do with this. Your education has no grafting power. Faith is the grafting power that has added you powerfully to a new group!

Your call to the ministry is another manifestation of the grafting power of faith. You originally belonged to a group of carpenters, tailors, doctors, teachers, lawyers, bankers, plumbers, computer workers and secular workers. The grafting power of faith has joined you to a completely different group.

I belonged to a group of medical doctors. Today, I have been grafted into a group of ministers of the gospel. When professors, physicians, gynaecologists, surgeons, neurologists, hospitalists and nocturnists are meeting, I am not found there. But when apostles, prophets, teachers, pastors and evangelists are gathering, I find my place. This is a miracle! I have no natural reason to belong to such a group. Faith has given me a new family. Faith has grafted me into a new group.

I predict that your faith is going to graft you in! You will soon be joined to a new group that you do not originally belong to. Perhaps, you belong to a group of uneducated and ignorant outsiders. Perhaps, you belong to a gang of wicked boys. God is grafting you into a new group. Perhaps you originally belong to the poorest and most deprived group of people on earth. Today, God is grafting you into an amazing group of prosperous, successful and blessed individuals.

Grafting faith is a wonderful thing that will change everything about your life. Keep stirring up your grafting faith. Grafting faith will really help you and give you favour in a new group. Grafting faith is your secret weapon of attachment!

Grafting faith comes by hearing and hearing comes by the word of God. The more you listen to preaching, the more you will be grafted in. Keep developing your faith by listening to even more preaching and teaching.

You will be grafted into an amazing group as you develop your faith.

CHAPTER 59

Faith Forces God's Hand to Perform Wonders

And blessed is she that believed: for there shall be a performance of those things which were told her from the Lord.

Luke 1:45

Faith Forces God's Hand to Perform Wonders

Blessed is she that believes! There will be a performance. There is always a performance for those who believe. There is no performance for those who do not believe.

Faith will force God's Hand to perform. Faith will compel God to act. Faith will cause God's commitment to your cause. Faith will invoke the power and presence in your affairs. Faith will make God perform wonders for you.

Faith is the key that will change your relationship with God. Keep developing your faith. Faith will make God perform wonders in your life. Faith is the secret of Mary and Elisabeth. They believed in the prophecy.

Faith comes by hearing and hearing comes by the word of God. The more you listen to preaching, the more your faith is built up! Keep developing your faith by listening even more to preaching and teaching.

You will notice that everyone performs according to what people think of them. When you think of the people that believe in you, you want to perform according to their expectations. If they expect something good from you, you want to perform those good things. If your children think you will bring them good presents, you want to perform accordingly.

That is why it is not good to accuse someone of evil when you are not sure of what you are saying. People perform according to your expectation. If a person feels you expect nothing from them, they do nothing! If a person feels you think they are pure, they try to live up to that purity. If they think you expect them to be immoral, they may fall easily into immorality. There is always a performance according to your faith.

God also performs according to our faith. Your faith pushes God's Hands to perform wonders. When God sees your great faith in His saving power, He is provoked to save you with mighty power.

Faith Secrets

All that you want from God will come through your faith. God will rise up and perform wonders for you again and again. It is time for you to become a man of faith.

Faith comes by hearing! Start hearing the right things and start believing in God. There will be a performance according to your faith. God is forced to perform according to your faith in Him. He cannot deny Himself!

CHAPTER 60

Faith Saves You from Perishing

That whosoever believeth in him should not perish, but have eternal life. For God so loved the world, that he gave his only begotten Son, that whosoever believeth in him should not perish, but have everlasting life. For God sent not his Son into the world to condemn the world; but that the world through him might be saved. He that believeth on him is not condemned: but he that believeth not is condemned already, because he hath not believed in the name of the only begotten Son of God.

John 3:15-18

Faith Secrets

To perish is to die, to suffer or be destroyed through violence or ruin. Today, Jesus offers salvation from perishing through faith in Him. Indeed, all of us were doomed to perish in the lake of fire. We were destined to be ruined and destroyed in hell. We were destined to violently perish in Gehenna. No human being on earth can deny that he is a sinner. No human being can deny that he deserves to violently and permanently perish in the lake of fire.

Today, you have escaped from this eternal prison by faith in God. It is not by works of righteousness but by faith in Jesus Christ. Your faith has saved you! Your works could not save you! Your good deeds did not save you! Building classrooms for your old school could not save you. Providing boreholes for your village could not save you. Setting up an NGO to help the poor could not save you. Having a good image in society could not save you.

This is why faith is so important. Faith saves you from perishing in hell! God is extremely wise. He has decided to use faith to determine those who will escape from perishing. Faith is something that is available to everybody. The rich, the poor, the educated, the idiot, the homeless, the Americans, the Africans and the Asians all have the same access to faith.

Faith is your master key to save you from perishing. Your faith is truly precious. It is your master key to saving you from violent, permanent ruin and destruction.

Faith is a wonderful key that will change everything about your life. Keep stirring up your faith. Faith will really help you and give you favour. Faith is your secret weapon! Faith comes by hearing and hearing comes by the word of God.

Keep developing your faith by listening even more to preaching and teaching.

You will have great favour with God as you develop your faith. Faith is the only thing that will work for you. Your faith is saving you from perishing!

CHAPTER 61

Faith Is Your Only Way to Please God

By faith Enoch was translated that he should not see death; and was not found, because God had translated him: for before his translation he had this testimony, that he pleased God. But without faith it is IMPOSSIBLE TO PLEASE HIM : for he that cometh to God must believe that he is, and that he is a rewarder of them that diligently seek him.

Hebrews 11:5-6

People are pleased by different things. Some women are pleased by men who care for them and give them security. Some men are pleased by women who offer them sexual pleasures. Some politicians are pleased by men who give them money.

Since people are pleased by different things, you are going to have to find out how to please the important people in your life. God has been kind to us and shown us what pleases Him. God is pleased by faith! When you please men you often do not please God. Pleasing men is often the furthest thing from pleasing God!

> For do I now persuade men, or God? or do I seek to please men? for if I yet pleased men, I should not be the servant of Christ.
>
> Galatians 1:10

In our hearts, we feel that God is pleased by moral excellence. We are naturally drawn to sin and wickedness. When we overcome our unholy urges, we feel we have pleased God. Unfortunately, none of our human standards are God's standards. God has already defined what pleases Him.

Look at the list of heroes of faith. What can you say about their moral uprightness? Almost every one of the heroes of faith showed the same signs of moral failure. Abraham offered up his wife to save his own life. Abraham had many wives. Many would frown on that today. Jacob had children with four women. If a pastor had children with four women today, I wonder if he would be accepted.

David had many wives and was clearly implicated in the murder of Uriah the Hittite. Solomon had a thousand wives. Today, Solomon would not be accepted as a good person. Noah had problems with drinking and also cursed one of his children.

Rahab, one of the heroes of faith, was a harlot by profession. Samson was a women's man.

The human idea of what pleases God cannot work with this list of failing human beings. That is why faith is so important.

God has defined what is important to Him. Faith is important to Him! Often, if you please one person you cannot please another. Often, if you please one person, the other will be displeased. You often have to choose whom you want to please.

Often, when you please God, you anger men.

Some people are also deluded into thinking that if they please *the society* they please God. Some people are also deluded into thinking that if they please *the majority* they are pleasing God.

Some people are also deluded into thinking that if they please their wives they please God. There is nothing further from the truth than that. The scripture below confirms the fact that pleasing your wife is very different from pleasing the Lord.

> But I would have you without carefulness. He that is unmarried careth for the things that belong to the Lord, how he may please the Lord: But he that is married careth for the things that are of the world, how he may please his wife.
>
> 1 Corinthians 7:32-33

It is time to please God! It is time to develop your faith. The more you listen to preaching and teaching the more your faith will grow. The more you listen to preaching and teaching, the more you will please God. The more obedient you are to the word of God, the more pleasing you will be to God. Faith is obedience and obedience if faith! The more you obey God, the more you please Him. Faith is your only way to please God.

CHAPTER 62

Faith Is a Powerful, Inexorable Creative Force

Through faith we understand that the worlds were framed by the word of God, so that things which are seen were not made of things which do appear.

Hebrews 11:3

The world was framed by the word of God. Faith created the world we live in. A short visit to the other planets would show you how different things are over there.

Planets, which have not experienced creation, are dark, void, lifeless and empty. Our sister planet, Venus, has a temperature of four hundred and fifty degrees Celsius. When the temperature on earth is just thirty-one degrees Celsius, human beings struggle with the heat. You can imagine what life on Venus is like. Venus is very hot indeed. You would dissolve in seconds after you arrive on Venus.

The atmospheric pressure on the planet Venus is the pressure you feel when you dive miles under water. Try diving to thirteen feet under water, and you will experience extreme pain in your ears. Imagine what it is like to be one mile below the surface of water. That is what it is like to be on Venus. Your head would burst open as soon as you landed on Venus. Please do not go there for a vacation.

Venus, which has not had the blessing of creation, experiences continuous volcanoes and earthquakes erupting across it. Venus also has rainfall but the rain is not water, but acid. If you were to arrive on Venus, you would experience lots of heavy acid rain. I do not think you would like that. Please do not plan to have your honeymoon on Venus!

The barren landscapes of Mars, Venus and Mercury show what it is like when the power of a creative force has not affected it. Today, we live on earth in the right atmospheric pressure and at the right temperature. We are happy to enjoy what God has created. Creative power is what makes it possible for human beings to exist. That creative power came from God, working through the powerful inexorable creative force of faith. Faith is an unstoppable, powerful inexorable force that creates things that never existed.

Through faith, you will be involved in creating things that have never existed. Your obedience to His word is your faith in action. By faith, God has used me to build churches that never existed before I came into the world.

Faith Secrets

By faith, God has used me to write books that never existed before I came into the world.

By faith, God has used me to create organizations that never existed before I came into the world. Through faith, God has used me to establish denominations of churches that never existed before I came into the world.

This is why faith is important. Whatever you do not have, can be created by the inexorable power of faith.

Your marriage, which does not exist, will be brought into existence by the inexorable creative power of faith. Your children, who do not exist today, will come into the world through the power of faith.

Do you see why faith is so important? Faith is an unstoppable force that will keep you walking with God.

Instead of questioning and doubting God's word, you must walk on in faith and trust the Word. As you step out in faith, you will see many things being created before your very eyes. Have faith in God! Walk by faith! Faith comes by hearing and hearing comes by the word of God. Your creative power comes as you hear the word of God. Keep coming to church! Listen to the messages over and over! Listen to old messages and new messages. Your words will become creative! Your words will be filled with faith!

Watch as many preaching videos as you can! Keep listening to messages at home, at school and at work. Listen to the word of God whilst you are walking and whilst you are working. It is your master key to the inexorable creative power of faith.

CHAPTER 63

Faith Accepts An Inheritance

By faith Abraham, when he was called to go out into a place which he should after receive for an inheritance, obeyed; and he went out, not knowing whither he went.

Hebrews 11:8

Faith Secrets

Abraham loved his inheritance. Abraham accepted his inheritance. Abraham was a man of faith.

Faith loves its inheritance. Faith flows towards its inheritance. Faith shamelessly possesses its inheritance. Faith believes in and takes over its spiritual inheritance. Faith loves it! Faith accepts riches as a provision from God. Faithless people don't easily accept their inheritance nor flow with it.

Some people feel the need to work for everything. Inheritance is not something you earn. Inheritance is something you receive and enjoy. It takes humility to receive things you did not work for.

There is also a spiritual inheritance that you must accept and flow in. What is a spiritual inheritance? A spiritual inheritance is an anointing, a gift or a grace you receive from an anointed person. Elisha received the anointing from Elijah. This was a spiritual inheritance. All that Elisha had to do was to walk on in the footsteps of Elijah and copy the methods of ministry that had worked for Elijah.

And it came to pass, when they were gone over, that Elijah said unto Elisha, Ask what I shall do for thee, before I be taken away from thee. And Elisha said, I pray thee, let a double portion of thy spirit be upon me.

2 Kings 2:9

Today, you may be walking in the footsteps of a great man of God. That is an inheritance. God is giving you an inheritance! There is no need to invent something new. You can take off in the ministry from a very high point. Some people are too proud to preach the same messages that have worked for years. They are too proud to walk by faith. Abraham had no difficulty in enjoying the inheritance God gave to him. Some people are so proud that they have to show the world how they labored for their own revelation. Abraham had no such difficulty. He simply flowed into the easy life of living by a solid inheritance.

I have often marveled at some of my sons and disciples in ministry who struggle to walk in the inheritance they have because they are part of my ministry. There are those who feel they must be original. They must let the congregation feel how close they are to God. They must hide the fact that they have read a book and listened to a message. When you behave like that you are not accepting the blessing of an inheritance.

Every house has its riches. My ministry has its riches in revelation, understanding, and knowledge. My ministry has its riches in books and teachings. It is the duty of my sons and disciples in the ministry to fully imbibe and use these books and revelations as a platform to grow deeper into God.

Instead of questioning and doubting God's inheritance for you, you must walk on in faith and trust the Word. As you step into your inheritance, you will see yourself moving forward very quickly.

Have faith in God! Walk by faith and receive your inheritance! Faith comes by hearing and hearing comes by the word of God. Keep coming to church. Listen to the messages over and over. Receive your inheritance now! Listen to old messages and new messages. Read the books God has placed in your hands. They are your inheritance!

Watch as many preaching videos as you can! That is your inheritance! Keep listening to messages at home, at school and at work. That is an inheritance for ministry! Listen to the word of God whilst you are walking and whilst you are working. It is your master key to the inexorable creative power of faith.

CHAPTER 64

Faith Will Offer the Excellent Sacrifice

By faith Abel offered unto God a more excellent sacrifice than Cain, by which he obtained witness that he was righteous, God testifying of his gifts: and by it he being dead yet speaketh.

Hebrews 11:4

Cain was rejected because his sacrifice to God was not excellent.

It is only when you have faith that you can offer an excellent sacrifice to God. Faith is obedience and obedience is faith! A sacrifice is to give up something you need, something you love and something you treasure to God. All through the Bible, you see people giving up important things so that they could serve the Lord.

Abraham made sacrifices to God! Isaac made sacrifices to God! Jacob made sacrifices to God! Solomon made sacrifices to God! Noah made sacrifices to God!

Sacrifice is only possible because you have faith. Your faith will enable you to make big sacrifices to God. Without faith you cannot give anything to God. To pay your tithe is a sacrifice. To make a big offering is a sacrifice. To throw some change into an offering bowl is not a sacrifice.

The very first conflict on earth came about because of different levels of faith. Abel and Cain had completely different levels of faith. When you have different levels of faith, you have different levels of sacrifice.

When a married couple has different levels of faith, they will often argue about what to do. I have watched as different couples had serious conflicts because they had different levels of faith. One wife believed in serving God and sacrificing her life for the ministry. The husband, who had a different level of faith, believed in giving his life to the secular world. These different levels of faith caused intense conflict.

A couple made one hundred thousand dollars profit from their business. Once again this couple had different levels of faith. The wife believed that they should give ten thousand dollars as their tithe. But the husband considered it absurd that they should put so much money in the offering. It is only by faith that you will make sacrifices to the kingdom of God. Those who make sacrifices because of politics, do so because of their belief in politics.

Faith Secrets

Abraham, Isaac, Jacob were men of faith! You will never amount to anything in God until you learn to make sacrifices. Your level of sacrifice reveals your faith! You will never be able to make any big sacrifice until you have faith in God.

You are accepted or rejected depending on your sacrifice.

Your level of sacrifice is important. Faith will enable you to give an excellent sacrifice. Through your sacrifice, your relationship with God will mount up into the highest levels.

Don't you want to have a great relationship with God?

Instead of fighting with the idea of sacrifice, develop your faith and no sacrifice will be too big for you to make to God. Have faith in God! Walk by faith! Raise the level of your sacrifice. Give your life as a sacrifice to Jesus. Pay your tithes as a sacrifice to God. Keep coming to church. Listen to the messages over and over. Listen to messages that make you give your life as a more excellent sacrifice to God.

Watch as many preaching videos as you can! Keep listening to messages at home, at school and at work. Listen to the word of God whilst you are walking and whilst you are working. You will willingly give your life as a living sacrifice to Jesus.

Faith loves sacrifices! Faith makes sacrifices! Faith pays tithes! Faith walks in giving! Faith goes on missions! Faith gives up everything for God! Faith makes a more excellent sacrifice! Faith works harder than everyone else! Faith makes a more excellent sacrifice!

CHAPTER 65

Faith Loves Adventure

By faith he sojourned in the land of promise, as in a strange country, dwelling in tabernacles with Isaac and Jacob, the heirs with him of the same promise:

Hebrews 11:9

Faith loves adventure! Faith is ready and happy to embark on the great adventure of serving God. God sent Abraham into a foreign land. He was asked to go somewhere without knowing where he was going. Abraham had no idea of where he was going. He had no idea of what he was going to do. If you want to serve God, you have to be like Abraham. You must love adventure! If you want to walk by faith, you have to be like Abraham, not knowing how things are going to turn out. A man of faith loves adventure.

When I married my wife, I knew that I was going on a journey of ministry. I did not know where I was going. I just had a vague idea in my heart that I needed to serve God. Thankfully, my wife was not averse to the idea of adventure, exploration and discovery. She accompanied me on the mysterious journey of ministry.

Serving God is the greatest adventure you can ever embark on. Faith embraces the adventure that comes with serving God. Your whole life becomes a series of explorations. You are on a quest to discover new things that God has for you.

When you walk by faith, you obey God and you will accept any adventure He leads you to.

If God has called you to the ministry, you must not marry someone who is not prepared to embark on an adventure. When you are on an adventure, you cannot answer many questions that are put to you. You cannot answer the questions because you do not know the answers. If Sarah had asked Abraham a lot of questions, he would have faltered. It would have seemed that he was hiding something from her.

The Great Commission is a great adventure. People who reject adventure reject the Great Commission. "Go ye into all the world and preach the gospel of Jesus Christ." Going into all the world is an adventure and involves great risk. If you want to serve God, make sure you ask your spouse if she is ready for the adventure of ministry.

Full-time ministry is a great adventure with lots of risks. People who do not embrace adventure will reject full-time ministry.

Going on missions to live in a foreign land is a great adventure.

Instead of living in a solid building, Abraham, Isaac and Jacob lived in tents. Every day that passed did not reduce the intensity of the adventure. The adventure continued throughout their lives. The wives of Abraham and Isaac were almost given away to other men. All that added spice to their adventure.

One day, I attended a service in which an evangelist gave a heart-wrenching testimony about how his wife left him. His wife had said to him, "I want to have a normal life. I want to have a normal husband. I want to have a man who comes home every day." She wanted him to stop travelling! She wanted him to stop preaching! She gave him an option to choose between herself and the ministry. He chose the ministry and he lost his wife.

If you do not embrace the reality of the adventurous journey of faith, you will struggle to walk with God and to serve Him.

CHAPTER 66

Faith Says "Yes"

By faith Abraham, when he was called to go out into a place which he should after receive for an inheritance, obeyed; and he went out, not knowing whither he went.

Hebrews 11:8

Faith Says "Yes"

Every calling blossoms, grows, matures, prospers and succeeds through faith. Every calling flourishes on your faith.

It is important to say, "Yes" when God calls you.

Some people say "No."

Most people say an indirect "No"! "Sure Lord, I'll be there. Just give me some time." "Lord, can we discuss this next week?"

You must say "Yes" to God!

Saying "Yes" is a very important spiritual step. Saying "Yes" is an important spiritual step of faith.

When Jairus requested that Jesus visit to raise his daughter from the dead, Jesus said "Yes". He went along with Jairus all the way to his house. Jesus healed Jairus' daughter in a powerful miracle service.

> And, behold, there cometh one of the rulers of the synagogue, Jairus by name; and when he saw him, he fell at his feet, And besought him greatly, saying, My little daughter lieth at the point of death: I pray thee, come and lay thy hands on her, that she may be healed; and she shall live. And Jesus went with him; and much people followed him, and thronged him.
>
> Mark 5:22-24

When the centurion asked for Jesus to come and visit his house, Jesus obliged and started the journey to the centurion's house. Jesus said "Yes" whenever He was asked to come and help.

> And a certain centurion's servant, who was dear unto him, was sick, and ready to die. And when he heard of Jesus, he sent unto him the elders of the Jews, beseeching him that he would come and heal his servant. And when they came to Jesus, they besought him instantly, saying, That he was worthy for whom he should do this: For he loveth our nation, and he hath built us a synagogue. Then Jesus went with them...
>
> Luke 7:2-6

Saying "Yes" is an important part of walking by faith. If Jesus had not said "Yes" all the time, most of the miracles of His ministry would not have happened.

Say "Yes" to the call of God.

Say "Yes" to people when they request for your help.

God will bless you as you say "Yes."

You must increase your faith so that you can always say "Yes."

Instead of saying "No" or "Maybe" you must start saying, "Yes." As you say "Yes" you will be drawn to higher levels of faith and miracles.

Have faith in God! Say "Yes" to God! Faith comes by hearing and hearing comes by the word of God. As you listen to the messages over and over, you will naturally find yourself saying "Yes" and flowing with the will of God.

Listen to messages in the Word. Watch as much preaching as you can! Keep listening to messages everywhere you go. You will soon be saying yes to God instead of "No", "Maybe," "Later," or "Let's discuss it next year."

CHAPTER 67

Faith Has An Unlimited Capacity for Visions

And the Lord answered me, and said, Write the vision, and make it plain upon tables, that he may run that readeth it. For THE VISION is yet for an appointed time, but at the end it shall speak, and not lie: though it tarry, wait for it; because it will surely come, it will not tarry. Behold, his soul which is lifted up is not upright in him: but the just shall live by his FAITH.

Habakkuk 2:2-4

Faith loves visions! A man of faith is excited to receive a vision from the Lord. All he will say is "Amen." A vision will not die in a man of faith. Every vision becomes real, blossoms, grows, matures, prospers and succeeds through faith.

Every calling flourishes through your faith.

When God calls you, He will give you a vision. God brought the Israelites out of Egypt with a clear vision of taking the Promised Land. Faith has a great capacity to accept the visions of God. The spies who were sent to spy out the land did not have the capacity to see how they would conquer the Promised Land. Because they had no faith, they could not understand the vision.

> And they brought up an evil report of the land which they had searched unto the children of Israel, saying, The land, through which we have gone to search it, is a land that eateth up the inhabitants thereof; and all the people that we saw in it are men of a great stature. And there we saw the giants, the sons of Anak, which come of the giants: and we were in our own sight as grasshoppers, and so we were in their sight.
>
> Numbers 13:32-33

The evil report that the spies brought was because of their lack of faith. The scriptures say they could not enter the Promised Land because they did not have faith. You must increase your capacity to accept the visions of God.

> **But with whom was he grieved forty years? was it not with them that had sinned, whose carcases fell in the wilderness? And to whom sware he that they should not enter into his rest, but to them that believed not? So we see that they could not enter in because of unbelief.**
>
> **Hebrew 3:17-19**

When God gives you a vision, make sure you share it with people of faith. Those who do not have faith will explain why the vision cannot be done. They will punch holes in your vision. They will fight you and oppose you because they do not have faith. Thousands of the Israelites died in the wilderness because they did not have faith.

If you allow men who have no faith to speak at meetings, they will kill the visions and ideas that God has given to you. You must develop your faith so that you can believe in visions.

Instead of questioning and doubting God's visions for you, you must walk on in faith and trust in God. As you step into God's visions for you, you will see yourself moving forward very quickly.

Visions are real! Have faith in God! The vision is real! Faith comes by hearing and hearing comes by the word of God. Develop your faith as you keep coming to church. Listen to the messages over and over. Listen to old messages and new messages. You will hear about how people believed in visions for their lives. Read the books God has placed in your hands. They will confirm the visions.

Set your heart on the visions that God shows you! Watch as many preaching videos as you can! Keep listening to messages at home, at school and at work. That is a vision for your ministry! Listen to the word of God whilst you are walking and whilst you are working. It is your master key to following the visions God gives to you.

When God gives you a vision, you must set your heart on it. You must meditate on it. You must think about it. You must imagine all the positive things about the vision. God will bring it to pass!

> And the man said unto me, Son of man, behold with thine eyes, and hear with thine ears, and SET THINE HEART UPON ALL THAT I SHALL SHEW THEE; for to the intent that I might shew them unto thee art thou brought hither: declare all that thou seest to the house of Israel.
>
> Ezekiel 40:4

CHAPTER 68

Faith Grows

We are bound to thank God always for you, brethren, as it is meet, because that YOUR FAITH GROWETH EXCEEDINGLY, and the charity of every one of you all toward each other aboundeth;

2 Thessalonians 1:3

When your faith grows, you will accomplish greater things. When your faith grows, you will obey the greater instructions of God.

Instead of allowing your faith to decrease, you must increase in faith and trust the Word. Faith grows!

Grow in faith! Believe God for bigger things. So how will my faith for ministry grow? How does faith grow? Faith grows by hearing! Faith comes by hearing and hearing and hearing!

So then faith cometh by hearing, and hearing by the word of God.

Romans 10:17

Faith comes by hearing and hearing comes by the word of God. Listen to the messages you love over and over. Listen to old messages and new messages. Read the books God has placed in your hands. They will increase your faith.

Watching Christian preaching videos will increase your faith. Keep listening to messages at home, at school and at work. That is how to grow your faith. Listen to the word of God whilst you are walking and whilst you are working. It is your master key to exceedingly great faith.

Faith also grows when you use it. The scripture teaches us that we gain by using what we have.

And it came to pass, that when he was returned, having received the kingdom, then he commanded these servants to be called unto him, to whom he had given the money, that he might know how much every man had GAINED BY TRADING.

Luke 19:15

Faith has a huge capacity for growth. Your faith grows as you use it! Your faith can grow exceedingly. Faith comes to those who hear the word of God. Over the years, you will notice that you are able to do certain things that you could not do before. You will overcome certain sins more easily as your faith grows.

Faith Secrets

As your faith grows, you will serve God with greater ease. Things that were impossible before will become easy to accomplish because your faith has grown. When your faith grows, the unstoppable force that accomplishes miracles also grows.

Some time ago, it would have taken Herculean effort for me to start a mission in a foreign country. Today, it is much easier to send missionaries into the world. It is easier to do these things because my faith has grown.

When I started out in ministry, I was unable to raise certain amounts of money for the work of God. As my faith grew, what took me one and a half years was accomplished in one hour. Why was that? My faith grew!

Faith grows! Some years ago, it took all my faith, all my effort, all my time and all my energy to get six hundred people to attend a crusade. Today, it is much easier to get six thousand people to attend a crusade. My faith for crusades has grown.

Some time ago, I would have been extremely tense, fearful and pressurized if I had to pray for the sick. Today, it is much easier for me to believe in miracles. My faith for the miracle ministry has grown.

Today marks the beginning of a great increase and growth of your faith! Therefore, it marks a great increase in your obedience. It marks a great increase in your accomplishments for God.

CHAPTER 69

Faith is the Trigger for the Supernatural

And when he was come into the house, the blind men came to him: and Jesus saith unto them, BELIEVE YE THAT I AM ABLE TO DO THIS? They said unto him, Yea, Lord. Then touched he their eyes, saying, According to your faith be it unto you. And their eyes were opened; and Jesus straitly charged them, saying, See that no man know it.

Matthew 9:28-30

Faith Secrets

All the miraculous events of Jesus' ministry were triggered by faith.

Faith is the trigger that sparks the supernatural in your life. Faith loves the supernatural. Faith is a key to the world of the supernatural. People who do not have faith will not see the supernatural or the miraculous.

As you walk in faith, the supernatural will take place in your life.

The Apostle Paul knew this trigger to a supernatural ministry. When he saw faith in people's eyes, he moved and miracles happened.

> **And there they preached the gospel. And there sat a certain man at Lystra, impotent in his feet, being a cripple from his mother's womb, who never had walked: THE SAME HEARD PAUL SPEAK: WHO STEDFASTLY BEHOLDING HIM, AND PERCEIVING THAT HE HAD FAITH TO BE HEALED, Said with a loud voice, Stand upright on thy feet. And he leaped and walked:**
>
> **Acts 14:7-10**

If you do not see faith, do not move! Minister to those who have faith. Minister to those who seem responsive to the ministry. Minister to those who seem to understand and receive.

A natural person cannot experience the miraculous. When Jesus came to His hometown, they asked questions, which were not out of order per se. They asked questions that anyone would ask. Who are His parents? Who are the brothers of Jesus? Who are the sisters of Jesus? Where does he live? What job did he do before He started his ministry? Was He really a carpenter? Even those of us who are alive today, know the answers to those questions. Anyone who considers the sensible, the rational, the reasonable and the logical realities will never see the supernatural.

If you analyze a man of God, you will not trigger the supernatural from his ministry. If you analyze me, you will never have faith in the supernatural. You will see my humanness, my weaknesses, my failings and my errors. That will not trigger the supernatural or the miraculous ministry that God has given me for you.

Today, many Bible schools dwell on the logical, reasonable facts concerning God, the Bible and Jesus Christ. As a result, the ministers who are trained in these Bible schools have very little faith and are unable to accomplish much for God. The trigger for the supernatural and the miraculous is faith and not logic or reason.

Do not attend a Bible school that rationalizes and analyses God's word! Attend a Bible school that imparts faith to you. Attend a Bible school that tells you how to do the work of ministry. Why study a "New Testament survey" after which you will not believe in the New Testament anymore? Why do an "Old Testament survey" after which you will find it difficult to believe in what is written in the Old Testament?

Instead of analysing, reasoning and rationalising God's word, start developing your trust in the promises of God. You will step into the supernatural by faith. You will trigger the miraculous by your faith.

Have faith in God! Walk by faith! Faith comes by hearing and hearing comes by the word of God. Keep coming to church. Listen to the messages over and over. Listen to old messages and new messages. Read the books God has placed in your hands. It will trigger the supernatural in your life.

Watch as many preaching videos as you can! Keep listening to messages at home, at school and at work. Listen to the word of God whilst you are walking and whilst you are working so that you trigger the supernatural in your life.

If your analyze Moses in a rational way, you may have to conclude that he was an authoritarian tyrant in the order of Julius Caesar or Napoleon. You would have to say that Moses was a dictator who wiped out all opposition to his strict and inflexible ideas. That sort of reasoning will cause you to miss out on the supernatural realities of who Moses really was.

If you analyze Joshua, you may see him as a brutal army general in the class of Hannibal or Alexander the Great. Indeed, if you take reasoning and logic too far, you will be unable to exercise faith and believe in supernatural things.

Faith is a trigger for the supernatural!

Do you want to see supernatural things? Do you want to have a supernatural ministry? Then remember that faith is the trigger for every supernatural event. Faith is the trigger for the miraculous! Analysis, logic and reasoning will not trigger the supernatural in your life.

CHAPTER 70

Faith Brings Glory into Your Life

Jesus saith unto her, Said I not unto thee, that, if thou wouldest believe, thou shouldest see the glory of God?

John 11:40

The glory of God was the raising of Lazarus from the dead. The showing forth of miracle power glorifies God and honours God. Jesus Christ was going to unleash the glory of God in front of Mary and Martha's family.

Faith brings the glory of God into your life and ministry. Many ministers of the gospel are like school teachers. They give a nice little lecture and they feel happy with themselves. If you want to have the glory of God in your ministry, you need to exercise faith. Faith will trigger the supernatural and the miraculous. The supernatural and the miraculous bring glory to God far more than any lecture can do.

I have always wondered why Moses was not allowed to enter the Promised Land. Moses was supposed to speak to a rock but he rather struck the rock with his rod.

God was not happy with Moses because he chose to operate in a lower level of miracle power. God is not happy with you when you choose to operate at a lower level of miracle power.

God is glorified when supernatural things happen. When a supernatural event happens, the wonder, the glory and the honour go to God because everyone knows that man could not have done it. God prefers ministries that have miracles, signs and wonders. Jesus was the ultimate example of ministry. His ministry was splattered with miracles and wonders. God prefers a man of God who demonstrates His power and glory. Your life may be shortened because you failed to walk in the kind of power that God has called you for.

> And the Lord spake unto Moses, saying, Take the rod, and gather thou the assembly together, thou, and Aaron thy brother, and SPEAK YE UNTO THE ROCK BEFORE THEIR EYES; and it shall give forth his water, and thou shalt bring forth to them water out of the rock: so thou shalt give the congregation and their beasts drink. And Moses took the rod from before the Lord, as he commanded him. And Moses and Aaron gathered the congregation together before the rock, and he said unto them, Hear now,

ye rebels; must we fetch you water out of this rock? And Moses lifted up his hand, and with his rod he smote the rock twice: and the water came out abundantly, and the congregation drank, and their beasts also.

And the Lord spake unto Moses and Aaron, BECAUSE YE BELIEVED ME NOT, TO SANCTIFY ME IN THE EYES OF THE CHILDREN OF ISRAEL, THEREFORE YE SHALL NOT BRING THIS CONGREGATION INTO THE LAND WHICH I HAVE GIVEN THEM.

Numbers 20:7-12

Be careful that you do not shorten your life and ministry by despising miracles, signs and wonders. Those who walk in mighty miracles and wonders have brought more glory to God than any other kind of ministry. Instead of questioning and doubting God's instructions for you, you must walk on in faith and trust in God. As you believe in God and obey Him, you will see the glory. Teaching and preaching is nice but God wants to see power demonstrations.

My prayer for you is that God will not reject you as He rejected Moses for operating in a lower level of miracle power.

Have faith in God! The glory will appear! This is the promise of Jesus. Faith comes by hearing and hearing comes by the word of God. Develop your faith as you keep coming to church. There must be miracle power and glory in your ministry. Listen to the messages over and over. Enter the supernatural and bring down the glory. Listen to old messages and new messages. Read the books God has placed in your hands. You are going to see the glory of God in your ministry. Your faith is rising! Glory is determined for you!

Watch as many preaching videos as you can! Keep listening to messages at home, at school and at work. It is possible to see the glory of God. Listen to the word of God whilst you are walking and whilst you are working. If you believe, you will see the glory of God.

CHAPTER 71

Faith Is the Pressure that You Apply

And he looked round about to see her that had done this thing. But the woman fearing and trembling, knowing what was done in her, came and fell down before him, and told him all the truth. And he said unto her, Daughter, thy faith hath made thee whole; go in peace, and be whole of thy plague.

Mark 5:32-34

A man who applies pressure is a man of faith!

The woman with the issue of blood is one great example of someone who pressed through to get her miracle. She applied a lot of pressure, pressed through the crowd and eventually touched Jesus. Jesus recommended her for her faith. *The manifestation of this woman's faith was the pressure that she applied until she made contact with Jesus.* All through the Bible those who received miracles were those who applied pressure. Faith is a pressure that you apply.

Blind Bartimaeus applied a lot of pressure on Jesus. He screamed and yelled until he got the attention of Jesus. Jesus did not rebuke blind Bartimaeus for shouting for him. Neither did he reprimand him for disturbing the peace.

Jesus simply acknowledged that blind Bartimaeus was a man of faith. Jesus said to blind Bartimaeus, "Go thy way. Thy faith has made thee whole." Jesus responded to the pressure that blind Bartimaeus applied on Him. Faith is the pressure that you apply.

There was a paralyzed man who was carried by his four friends. They broke into a man's house through the roof and presented the paralyzed man to Jesus Christ. Jesus did not call the police to arrest them for breaking into the house. Jesus did not present them with a bill for spoiling the roof. Jesus simply acknowledged that they were men of faith. When Jesus saw their faith, He said, "Your sins are forgiven." Jesus was acknowledging the pressure that they had applied on Him to receive their healing. Jesus equated pressure with faith. Faith is the pressure that you apply.

On the other hand, Jesus met a man who had been ill by the Pool of Bethesda for thirty-eight years. This man was not able to apply enough pressure to receive his miracle. Perhaps, he was phlegmatic. Jesus healed this man but this time, did not commend him for his faith. This man was not healed by his faith but by the compassion of Jesus.

Faith is the pressure you apply. Faith loves to apply pressure. Persevering people receive the benefits of faith.

Faith Secrets

It is time to apply pressure to receive what God has given to you. Faith comes by hearing. What has God promised you? Has He promised to give you church growth? Has He promised you an international ministry? Has He promised you a healing ministry? Has He promised you a husband or a wife? It is time to apply pressure so that you receive what God has for you.

Instead of questioning and doubting God's word, you must apply pressure until you receive it.

It is true that faith is the pressure that you apply. Faith comes by hearing and hearing comes by the word of God. Develop your faith as you keep coming to church. Listen to the messages over and over. Listen to old messages and new messages. Read the books God has placed in your hands. Soon you will be applying pressure on the gates of heaven. The pressure you apply will convert your defeat into victory.

Watch as many preaching videos as you can! Listen to the Machaneh[1]. Keep listening to messages at home, at school and at work. Listen to the word of God all the time. I see you applying pressure before the throne room. Soon, your desires will be delivered to you on a silver platter.

---

1. *"The Machaneh" is a collection of preaching and teaching camp messages by the author, Bishop Dag Heward-Mills. It is available on podcast and at daghewardmillsaudio.org*

CHAPTER 72

Faith Is Not in a Hurry

Therefore thus saith the Lord God, Behold, I lay in Zion for a foundation a stone, a tried stone, a precious corner stone, a sure foundation: he that believeth shall not make haste.

Isaiah 28:16

Faith Secrets

He that believeth shall not make haste. This means that he that believeth, shall never be in a hurry! He that believeth shall not be flustered! He that believeth shall not be anxious! Faith is not in a hurry. Faith does not need to hurry. Faith is not flustered or anxious about anything.

In a vision, a man of God saw Jesus walking on the beach. Jesus was not walking slowly. Neither was He hurrying up. He was walking at a steady stable pace. One of the lessons he was to learn from that vision was that Jesus was not in a hurry.

He that believeth shall not make haste! Jesus does not and will never panic! Jesus is not desperate! Neither should you be. God will do it in His time.

When you walk by faith, you will never be desperate or anxious. God will do what He will do. There is no need to risk everything so that you can do things faster and faster. God will make all things beautiful in His time.

He hath made every thing beautiful in his time: also he hath set the world in their heart, so that no man can find out the work that God maketh from the beginning to the end.

Ecclesiastes 3:11

There is no need to drive a certain kind of car this year or live in a certain type of house this year. There is no need to impress anyone about what you have achieved. God will make all things beautiful in His time.

Loans and debts are some of the big manifestations of faithless, hurrying people. The rush to belong, the rush to wear a Rolex watch and the rush to drive the best kind of car are not manifestations of faith at all. Indeed, he that believeth shall not make haste. He that believeth does not need to run around impressing anyone.

It is time to develop your faith and believe that God will give you everything you need. As you listen to the word of God, you become surer of yourself. You will not need to rush into loans, debts and fake prosperity.

Not keeping the Sabbath and not resting is another manifestation of faithlessness. He that believeth shall not make haste. When you have faith in God you will be able to rest. You will not need to use your resting day for work.

For we which have believed do enter into rest, as he said, As I have sworn in my wrath, if they shall enter into my rest: although the works were finished from the foundation of the world.

Hebrews 4:3

Faith loves rest. God rested after six days. Always remember that God's punishment for not resting is death.

Ye shall keep the sabbath therefore; for it is holy unto you: every one that defileth it shall SURELY BE PUT TO DEATH: for whosoever doeth any work therein, that soul shall be cut off from among his people.

Exodus 31:14

Instead of running around on the Sabbath day, you will rest in God and not be in a hurry. You will believe that God's pace of blessing you is good enough. If God wants to do it, He will do it and in His time

A man of faith is not in a hurry. Faith is real! Have faith in God! Faith comes by hearing and hearing comes by the word of God. Develop your faith as you keep coming to church. Listen to the messages over and over. Listen to old messages and new messages. Read the books God has placed in your hands. They will confirm that you do not need to hurry.

Watch as many preaching videos as you can! Keep listening to messages at home, at school and at work. You will surely start resting in God. Listen to the word of God whilst you are walking and whilst you are working. This is the master key of a restful life in God where you are not in a hurry. A man of faith is not in a hurry.

CHAPTER 73

Faith Is a Mighty Weapon

Above all, taking the shield of faith, wherewith ye shall be able to quench all the fiery darts of the wicked.

Ephesians 6:16

Faith is a weapon that non-Christians do not have!

Faith is listed as one of the spiritual weapons we have been given. It is important to fight your spiritual battles with faith. The weapons of our warfare are mighty through God.

You must ward off evil spirits by your faith. You must make declarations and fight in the spirit realm through faith. Faith is a weapon that unbelievers do not have. All the demons of hell are hoping that you will not rise up and use your faith. They are hoping that you will question, analyze and rationalize the word of God.

Instead of questioning and doubting God's word, you must walk in faith and trust in God. If you do not do that, satan will have the upper hand.

Faith is a real weapon. Have faith in God! Faith comes by hearing and hearing comes by the word of God. Develop your faith by listening to preaching and teaching all the time. Read the books God has placed in your hands. They will multiply the word of God in you and increase your faith.

What is the difference between you and an unbeliever? Faith! The Israelites crossed the Red Sea successfully because they had faith. Their secret weapon against the Egyptians was faith. The Egyptians also tried to cross the Red Sea but it did not work. What the Egyptians lacked was faith.

> By faith they passed through the Red sea as by dry land: WHICH THE EGYPTIANS ASSAYING TO DO WERE DROWNED.
>
> Hebrews 11:29

Build a huge shield of faith by watching as many preaching videos as you can! Keep listening to teaching messages at home, at school and at work. You are developing the greatest weapon of war. Listen to the word of God whilst you are walking and whilst you are working. It is your master key to building a huge shield of faith. Through faith, you will fight demons and overcome the devil.

Some years ago, I was involved in casting out devils from a possessed person. We spent about eight hours praying and binding the devil. By evening we were exhausted from praying, binding and casting. Suddenly, a senior Christian with greater faith entered the room where we were casting the demon out of the demon-possessed person. He commanded the devil to come out with one word and the person was delivered.

He reprimanded us for not having faith in our prayers and ability to cast out demons. He then declared that our prayers were enough and that we had to believe that our command of faith had worked. Truly, the possessed person was suddenly set free.

I never forgot that lesson. Never put faith aside! You need to add faith to your prayers. Faith is a major weapon that God has given us. You put faith aside at your own peril. Faith is a mighty weapon!

CHAPTER 74

Faith is Mysterious in Its Working

Likewise must the deacons be grave, not doubletongued, not given to much wine, not greedy of filthy lucre; Holding THE MYSTERY OF THE FAITH in a pure conscience.

1 Timothy 3:8-9

Faith is mysterious in its working. You cannot easily understand how faith works. Indeed, faith truly works! But it works in a mysterious way! If you cannot understand the way something works, then it is mysterious. When someone is healed by faith, it is difficult to understand how the healing actually took place.

Faith is a mystery. Do not beat yourself up because you do not understand how exactly faith works. We accept many mysterious things and use them all the time. Most of us do not know how mobile phones and televisions work. But we are comfortable using them all the time.

It is because faith is mysterious that this book has so many chapters. Faith is an element that is not so easy to define. Faith is much more than an attitude of trust. Faith is not just a set of beliefs. Faith is an unstoppable force. Faith is obedience and obedience is faith! Faith is also the victory that overcomes the world. Faith is many things. Ultimately, faith is mysterious!

NOTES

Chapter 11

Semper Paratus Definition Retrieved from: https://www.merriam-webster.com/dictionary/semper%20paratus. May 2019

Chapter 39

Excerpt retreived from: https://www.ynetnews.com/articles/0,7340,L-4999815,00.html. May 2019

Chapter 44

"*Bamboo Tree*" retrieved from: https://www.linkedin.com/pulse/success-like-chinese-bamboo-tree-patience-patrick-karuri. May 2019

Chapter 49

Excerpt retrieved from: https://woleacmilan.files.wordpress.com/2014/02/bible-study-link.pdf. May 2019

Chapter 50

Excerpt retrieved from: http://redeemedofchristchapel.org/champions-daily-vitamin-october-292012/